Praise for *Letters to My Palestinian Neighbor*

"A clarion call, not to arms but to empathy . . . a profound and original book, the work of a gifted thinker . . . [an] urgent and heartfelt message."
—Daphne Merkin, *Wall Street Journal*

"One of the best one-volume introductions to the conflict between Israel and the Palestinians."
—*The Atlantic*

"The tantalizing proposition of Halevi's book, never belabored but always peeking from between the lines, is that faith might unite these two warring tribes whereas reason only fanned the flames of discord."
—*Tablet* magazine

"Yossi Klein Halevi wants to extend an olive branch to his Palestinian neighbors, and does so, in his incredibly compelling and heartfelt book *Letters to My Palestinian Neighbor*."
—*Jerusalem Post*

"Halevi's book, a collection of letters addressed to his Palestinian counterparts, functions as a new attempt at discourse that starts on a grassroots level. His language is beautiful. So is the idea behind the book: radical, unceasing empathy for the other—combined with an unadulterated, unmitigated dedication to one's own people and one's own land."
—*Business Insider*

"By providing an honest, soulful, and balanced recap of two emotional narratives, *Letters to My Palestinian Neighbor* has given us a spiritual roadmap, if not to peace, then at least to hope."     —*Jewish Journal*

"The most insightful description of this deep-rooted conflict—from the Israeli perspective—which I have ever read. . . . A master linguist, Yossi Klein Halevi has voiced the hopes and fears of many Israelis, as well as many Zionists in the diaspora."
—*London Jewish Chronicle*

"Yossi Klein Halevi is a very brave man. . . . Halevi's new book, *Letters to My Palestinian Neighbor*, builds on what he discovered in his earlier quest: that this spiritual common ground could lead to mutual acceptance. I hope the book reaches its intended audiences both in the Middle East and around the world."
—*Globe and Mail*

"Refreshingly honest. . . . In explaining Israel to the Palestinians, [Halevi] appeals to a certain ideal, a higher ambition, a sense of wonder and beauty."
—*The Forward*

"Eloquent and important."     —*Jewish Boston*

"Halevi combines the sharp eye of a journalist and refined mastery of disciplined, precise writing with the knowledge and temperament of a wizened scholar of Jewish history. . . . Halevi's writing is both lyrical and taut. Every page, it seems, features a nugget of compacted history or condensed theology. . . . It is precisely because of his reputation as a principled, thoughtful, unapologetic advocate for Israel that the sincere, respectful, and hopeful tone of his plea is so poignant."

—Mordechai Ben-Dat, *Canadian Jewish News*

"The best book that you will read this year—about Israel, and about Judaism—is *Letters to My Palestinian Neighbor*."

—Religion News Service

"Powerful and eloquent. . . . Capturing the enduring Jewish love of the land of Israel and the magic as well as the dilemmas of Zionism, the letters are highly compelling. There is no one better suited to tell the story of Israel and the Jewish people than Halevi—and not just to Palestinians. An inspired reading of the Israeli soul, *Letters to My Palestinian Neighbor* should be recommended to non-Jews and Jews alike." —*Commentary* magazine

"When it came to Israel and Palestine, to Muslims and Jews, I had long come to feel that there couldn't be much new under the sun. How happy I am to be proven so wrong. Halevi's book is a gift and a challenge, a gorgeously composed, deeply personal accomplishment animated by this simple gesture: I will share my convictions, because I wish for you to share yours. Then, and only then, can we find a durable peace. These letters overflow with faith, conveyed by Halevi's sincerity and humility. You, like me, may find yourself disagreeing from time to time, and even strongly so. But you will never find yourself unmoved. There are, of course, always those who are willing to talk, if only we'd listen. What Halevi demonstrates is far more unusual: there are also those who are willing to listen, if only we'd talk."

—Haroon Moghul, author of *How to Be a Muslim: An American Story*

"A powerful, challenging, and deeply moving plea for human understanding across one of the most tragic divides in modern politics."

—Rabbi Lord Jonathan Sacks

"*Letters to My Palestinian Neighbor* conveys the urgency and poetry of the Israeli story in a way that is accessible to any reader. I hope everyone will read these beautiful letters—Palestinians and Jews and anyone else interested in understanding who the Jews are and why we returned home."

—Natan Sharansky, Chairman of the Executive, Jewish Agency for Israel

"Halevi . . . offers a poetic and moving account of 'my experience as occupier' that asserts Israel's legitimacy and evokes its emotional importance for Jews but refuses to gloss over its flaws . . . [a] heartfelt, empathetic plea for connection and mutual acknowledgement."

—*Publishers Weekly*

Letters to My Palestinian Neighbor

ALSO BY YOSSI KLEIN HALEVI

*Like Dreamers*
*At the Entrance to the Garden of Eden*
*Memoirs of a Jewish Extremist*

# Letters to
# My Palestinian
# Neighbor

# Yossi Klein
# Halevi

HARPER **PERENNIAL**

NEW YORK • LONDON • TORONTO • SYDNEY • NEW DELHI • AUCKLAND

HARPER ● PERENNIAL

HarperCollins books may be purchased for educational, business, or sales
promotional use. For information, please email the Special Markets De-
partment at SPsales@harpercollins.com.

FIRST HARPER PERENNIAL EDITION PUBLISHED 2019.

*Designed by William Ruoto*

Library of Congress Cataloging-in-Publication Data has been applied for.

ISBN 978-0-06-284492-7 (pbk.)

24 25 26 27 28  LBC  15 14 13 12 11

*For Abdullah Antepli and Michael Oren,*
*my partners, my brothers*

# Contents

# A Note to the Reader

For the last five years, I have been privileged to co-direct, together with Imam Abdullah Antepli of Duke University, the Muslim Leadership Initiative (MLI), an educational program teaching about Judaism and Israel to young emerging Muslim American leaders. So far MLI has brought over a hundred participants to the Jerusalem campus of the Shalom Hartman Institute, Israel's preeminent center for pluralistic Jewish research and education, which sponsors MLI and where I serve as a fellow.

This book is, in part, a result of that project. Many of the issues raised in the following pages are an outgrowth of intense study sessions and informal conversations in which I've been engaged with Imam Abdullah and my other friends in MLI.

This book is an attempt to explain the Jewish story and the significance of Israel in Jewish identity to Palestinians who are my next-door neighbors. One of the main obstacles to peace is an inability to hear the other side's story. And so I am offering this book in

Arabic translation for free downloading. Here is the link: letterstomyneighbor.com

I invite Palestinians—as well as others throughout the Arab and Muslim worlds—to write me, at that same link, in response to any issue raised in this book. I will try to respond to every letter, no matter how challenging, that is written in a spirit of engagement. My intention is to initiate a public conversation on our shared future in the Middle East.

In a previous book, *At the Entrance to the Garden of Eden*, I wrote about a journey I undertook into Palestinian society. That journey was an attempt to understand something of the faith and experiences of my neighbors. This book is a kind of sequel: an attempt to explain to my neighbors something of my faith and experiences as an Israeli.

This book is an invitation to a conversation, in which both sides disagree on the most basic premises. And so I am writing to you, a Palestinian neighbor whom I don't yet know, with the hope that we may undertake a journey of listening to each other.

Letters to My Palestinian Neighbor

# The Wall between Us

Dear Neighbor,

I call you "neighbor" because I don't know your name or anything personal about you. Given our circumstances, "neighbor" may be too casual a word to describe our relationship. We are intruders in each other's dreams, violators of each other's sense of home. We are living incarnations of each other's worst historical nightmares. Neighbors?

But I don't know how else to address you. I once believed that we would actually meet, and I am writing to you with the hope that we still might. I imagine you in your house somewhere on the next hill, just beyond my porch. We don't know each other, but our lives are entwined.

And so: neighbor.

We live on opposite sides of a concrete wall that cuts through the landscape we share. I live in a neighborhood called French Hill in East Jerusalem, and my apartment is in the last row of houses, which you see as steplike structures built into the hillside.

From my apartment, I can just barely see the checkpoint you must cross—if you have a permit at all—to enter Jerusalem. But I sense the checkpoint's all-pervading presence. Sometimes my early-morning routine of meditation and prayer is disrupted by the prolonged honking of frustrated drivers lining up before the checkpoint. Maybe you have been caught in that desperate line.

Sometimes I see smoke rising over your hill. Black smoke, I've long since learned, can mean burning tires, accompanied by young people throwing rocks at soldiers. Then there is white smoke—soldiers firing tear gas. How do you manage, if at all, to preserve a measure of normal life?

As a Palestinian, you are denied the rights of citizenship that I enjoy as an Israeli. The ongoing disparity between your hill and mine challenges my deepest self-understanding and moral commitments as a Jew and an Israeli. Ending that disparity is one reason why I support a two-state solution.

It is just before dawn. I am in my study, facing your

hill. The muezzin calls, softly, as if reluctant to disturb the night. I wrap myself in a white prayer shawl and sit cross-legged on a meditation pillow. I touch my forehead to the ground, a nod to the call to prayer coming from across the way. In my most intimate conversation with God, I am hoping to speak to you.

A pale sun rises over the desert beyond the wall. I bind my arm with the black straps of tefillin, fasten a small black box on my forearm, facing my heart, another on my forehead. Heart and mind bound in devotion. Inside the boxes are biblical verses, including the seminal Jewish prayer proclaiming God's oneness: "Hear, Israel, the Lord our God is One." Or as the Qur'an puts it: "He is the One God, God the Eternal, the Uncaused Cause of all being."

Clearly visible outside my window, in a far corner of the sand-colored expanse, is an incongruous patch of blue: the Dead Sea. And just beyond, the hills of Jordan. I imagine myself merging into the vastness, a part of the Middle East—

But the wall restores me to reality, to the constriction just beyond my porch.

Once, before the wall was built, before so much else that went wrong, I tried to get to know you. In late 1998, in what seems like another lifetime—truly another century—I set out on a pilgrimage into Islam and Christianity, the faiths of my neighbors in the Holy Land. I went as a religious Jew seeking not so much to understand your theology as to experience something of your devotional life. I wanted to learn how you pray, how you encounter God in your most intimate moments.

My goal was to see whether Jews and Muslims could share something of God's presence, could be religious people together in this of all places, where God's Name is so often invoked to justify abomination. I wanted to learn to feel at home in a mosque, to see in Islam not threat but spiritual opportunity. To hear in the muezzin's call exactly what it is intended to be: a summons to awakening.

In Judaism, there is one sin for which not even the fast of Yom Kippur can atone: desecrating God's Name. Only a religious person, misusing or acting unjustly in the Name of God, can be guilty of that offense. The interfaith encounter, I believe, sanctifies God's Name. Interacting with believers of different faiths creates religious humility, recognition that truth and holiness aren't confined to any one path. I cherish Judaism as my language of intimacy with God; but God speaks many languages.

I longed to celebrate those multiple conversations,

to touch something of God's expanse. That was my intention as I entered the world of Islam.

I was privileged to be admitted, in several mosques, into the line of devotion, joining the Muslim choreography of prayer, the immersion of the body in worship. I learned that the experience of surrender begins with the formation of the line itself, aligning shoulder to shoulder with those of your neighbor on either side. And then the sacred movement: Bow, return, prostrate, stand. Repeat: until you feel your body turning to water, a particle in a great wave of prayer that began long before your birth and will continue long after your death.

Coexistence in the Holy Land is often ensured by mutual separation. The four quarters of the Old City of Jerusalem—Muslim, Jewish, Christian, Armenian—reinforce the message: Safety is measured by the distance between us.

My journey was a violation of the coexistence of distance, an insistence on the possibility of intimacy.

As part of my exploration of Islam, I was invited by friends to the Gaza refugee camp Nusseirat. In 1990, I had served there as a soldier, patrolling its narrow lanes. Teenagers throwing broken bottles and crowbars chanted, *"Amnon b'salem aleik"*—Amnon sends you regards—referring to Amnon Pomerantz, an army reservist who had made a wrong turn into El-Bureij, the neighboring refugee camp, was surrounded by a mob, and was burned alive.

A decade later, I returned to Nusseirat as a pilgrim. Sheikh Abdul-Rahim was the elderly leader of a small mosque of Sufis, mystics who emphasize the work of the heart. The sheikh welcomed me into his little mosque, built across from a cemetery to caution worshippers against frivolity. Initially, the sheikh tried to convert me to Islam, asking me to raise a finger and repeat after him the words of the Shahada, the Muslim testimony of faith. I explained that I had come to learn how my Muslim neighbors served God, but was content within my own faith. The sheikh was not appeased: There was no other way to God, he said, than through the Prophet.

Then, abruptly, the sheikh led me across the road to the cemetery. We entered the mausoleum of his teacher and stood in silence. He took my hand, and we shared the camaraderie of mortality.

I returned a few months later. This time Sheikh Abdul-Rahim smiled at me and put his hand on his heart. "Ever since you went into the tomb and put your hand in mine," he said, "I have considered you one of my own. All my students, Muslim or Jew, are in my heart."

By the end of my yearlong journey I had come to love Islam. I cherished its fearless heart, especially in the face of death. Westerners often try to evade an encounter with one's own mortality. Not so Muslims. I learned that Islam has the uncanny ability to impart in its believers—from the simplest to the most sophisticated—a frank awareness of one's own impermanence.

Sometimes, in political arguments with Palestinians, I would be told: Why are we arguing about who owns the land, when in the end the land will own us both? The identical expression exists in my tradition, too. The courage to embrace transience could help create a religious language of peace between our peoples, a basis for political flexibility, for letting go of absolutist claims.

I tell you all this, neighbor, because I assume that, like most Palestinians I've known, you are a religious person, and if not entirely observant, still a believer. My journey into your faith was an attempt to learn a religious language for peace. One reason, I believe, that the well-intentioned efforts of diplomats have failed so far is that they tend to ignore the deep religious commitments on both sides. For peace to succeed in the Middle East, it must speak in some way to our hearts.

And so I address you, one person of faith to another.

However differently we express it, that faith shares

an essential worldview: that the unseen is ultimately more real than the material, that this world is not a random construct but an expression, however veiled, of a purposeful creation. That we are not primarily bodies but souls, rooted in oneness. For me, the only notion more ludicrous than the existence of a Divine being that created and sustains us is the notion that this miracle of life, of consciousness, is coincidence.

I traveled in Palestinian society not only to learn about your devotional lives but also to glimpse something of this conflict through your eyes. To force myself open to the Palestinian tragedy: the shattering of a people whose organizing principle is now dislocation and whose most significant anniversaries are humiliating defeats.

I tried as best I could to step out of my own narrative and confront Palestinian historical attachments and the wrongs done by my side against yours. I met people whose homes had been destroyed by Israel because they built without a permit—permits the Jerusalem municipality has made difficult for Palestinians to obtain in the first place. I listened to your stories, read Palestinian histories and memoirs and poetry. Your narrative came to haunt me. Not that I ever lost my love for the Jewish return home—as we Jews put it—

which I cherish as a story of persistence and courage and, above all, faith. But I could no longer ignore your counter-story of invasion, occupation, and expulsion. Our two narratives now coexisted within me, opposing versions of the same story.

For many years we in Israel ignored you, treated you as invisible, transparent. Just as the Arab world denied the right of the Jews to define themselves as a people deserving national sovereignty, so we denied the Palestinians the right to define themselves as a distinct people within the Arab nation, and likewise deserving national sovereignty. To solve our conflict, we must recognize not only each other's right to self-determination but also each side's right to self-definition.

Many Israelis have now come to accept the legitimacy of your people's right to national self-definition. After the first intifada, the Palestinian uprising in the late 1980s, many Israelis of my generation became convinced that the Israeli Left had been correct all along in warning that the occupation was a disaster—for us as well as you. The price for implementing our historic claim to all of the land between the Jordan River and the Mediterranean Sea, we realized, was too high. We could not remain a democratic state with ethical Jewish values if we became a permanent occupier of your people, nor did we want to. I didn't return home to deny another people its own sense of home. I hope you will hear me when I tell you I have no intention of denying your claim or your pain.

Many Israelis, of course, continued to insist that all justice belongs to our side, that you have no real historical case. But it was then that a significant number began to feel differently. A camp of "guilty Israelis" emerged. We believed that the onus was on Israel as the occupier to reach out to the Palestinians with a serious peace offer. For that reason, we supported Israeli prime minister Yitzhak Rabin when he shook hands with Yasser Arafat on the White House lawn on September 13, 1993, officially launching the Oslo peace process.

And then, in September 2000, came the second intifada. Thousands of Israelis were killed or wounded in our streets—and thousands more in your streets. The skeletons of exploded buses became a part of the Israeli landscape. The tragedies blurred, but here is one that remains distinct for me: A suicide bomber struck the café near my office in Jerusalem and killed a father and daughter, on the literal eve of her wedding; the next day, the wedding guests gathered for her funeral. I had a connection to the family and visited the house of mourning. The grieving wife and mother assumed the role of comforter, reassuring all who came to her with faith and determination. It was then I knew that nothing would ever uproot the Jewish people from this land again.

My wife, Sarah, and I were raising two teenagers in those years. Every morning I made sure to kiss them good-bye, wondering if I would see them again. Both repeatedly found themselves in proximity to terror attacks. One thirteen-year-old boy, Koby Mandell, whom my son, Gavriel, knew from summer camp, was stoned to death; Koby's body, discovered in a cave, was so disfigured that only his DNA could identify him.

Israelis and Palestinians deeply disagree about who is to blame for the collapse of the peace process, and no doubt we will continue to argue the point for years to come. Most Israelis, myself included, believe that our leaders at the time tried to make peace, while your leaders rejected compromise and turned instead to terrorism, to undermine Israeli will and extract more concessions. No matter how much you may disagree with the Israeli narrative of why the Oslo process failed, you cannot understand Israelis today without accounting for how profoundly that narrative has shaped our worldview and our policies.

The second intifada is the moment most of us guilty

Israelis lost faith in the peaceful intentions of the Palestinian leadership. And not just because of the terrorism. We lost faith because the worst wave of terrorism in our history came *after* Israel had made what we considered a credible offer—two offers, actually—to end the occupation. At Camp David in July 2000, Prime Minister Ehud Barak became the first Israeli leader to accept a Palestinian state on the West Bank and in Gaza, with Palestinian neighborhoods in East Jerusalem as its capital. Israel would have committed to uprooting dozens of settlements and removing tens of thousands of settlers from their homes. There was no wall then, and any barrier built would have been a normal border, separating sovereign Israel from sovereign Palestine. The injustices that are inevitably a part of occupation would have ended. But Arafat rejected the offer, without presenting a counteroffer.

After those failed Camp David talks, Israelis and Palestinians argued about whether Israel had really made a serious offer. But then, six months later, in December 2000, President Bill Clinton presented his own peace plan, in which Barak's Camp David offer of around 91 percent of the territory was upped to 95 percent, with compensatory land swaps and a road cutting through Israeli territory to connect the West Bank and Gaza. Once again, Barak said yes, and Arafat said no. Later, Clinton blamed Arafat for the collapse of the peace process.

This was the shattering moment for many Israelis who believed in the possibility of resolving the conflict. I know Israelis who had devoted their careers to convincing their fellow citizens that the Palestinian leadership wanted peace with Israel, that we only had to make a credible offer and your side would naturally agree. The tragedy for the Israeli Left was that it actually succeeded in convincing a large part of our public to trust its approach. And then the peace process literally blew up in our faces.

In 2008, Israeli prime minister Ehud Olmert offered Palestinian leader Mahmoud Abbas the equivalent of full withdrawal from the territories, with land swaps. Abbas didn't respond. Today, ordinary Israelis who desperately want to live normal lives in a normal country at peace with its neighbors regard those leftists who still insist that Palestinian leaders want peace as delusional.

However horrifying the violence of the second intifada, its underlying motive was no less unsettling for Israelis: a denial of the Jewish people's right to exist as a sovereign nation in any part of the land we share, a denial of the idea that this is a land that needs to be shared by two peoples. We experienced the terrorism as an expression of a deeper pathology: an intention to destroy the Jewish presence in this land. A revolt not against occupation but against Israel's existence.

I've heard Palestinians say that they have no choice but to fight the occupation with violence. Israelis see an opposite dynamic: From our perspective, it's not the occupation that creates terror but terror that prolongs the occupation, by convincing Israelis that no matter what we do, in the end the terrorism against us will persist. That, after all, is what happened when Israel withdrew from Gaza in 2005, uprooting all its settlements and army bases. Yet thousands of rockets were fired for years afterward into Israeli neighborhoods along the border.

Palestinian leaders never stop telling their people that Israel has no historic legitimacy as a state. Those leaders have convinced us that this isn't a conflict, ultimately, about borders and settlements and Jerusalem and holy places. It is about our right to be here, in any borders. Our right to be considered a people. An indigenous people.

The withering of the Israeli Left transformed my country's politics for a generation. With the violent collapse of the Oslo process, the Right came back to power. The Israeli peace camp, which in the 1990s would summon hundreds of thousands of demonstrators into the streets, could now barely manage to rouse a few thousand.

Many Israelis of course understand that our side amply shares the blame for reaching this terrible impasse between our two peoples. For example, we continued to build in the settlements during the Oslo process, undermining your people's confidence in our commitment to a solution and reinforcing Palestinians' sense of helplessness. But when the decisive moment came to end the conflict, we saw our leaders saying yes and Palestinian leaders saying no.

I cite all this because it is the moment that changed Israeli society, that changed me. It explains how I can live with the moral burden of the occupation. How I can live with the wall outside my window.

My travels within Palestinian society ended. That became too dangerous: Israelis entering territory controlled by the Palestinian Authority risked being lynched. Finally Israel forbade its citizens from entering those areas. The relationships I'd formed with Palestinians faded.

As the human bombs detonated in the early 2000s, I, like most Israelis, backed the construction of a barrier separating the West Bank from Israel, your hill and mine. It was a desperate attempt to stop the unbearable ease with which suicide bombers crossed from the

West Bank into sovereign Israel, boarded our buses, and entered our cafés.

And it worked. With the construction of the barrier, the wave of suicide bombings ended. I see in that barrier a way of ensuring the safety of my children, my ability to survive in the Middle East. And so I find myself grateful to the wall I despise. Because I feel I have no choice.

The second intifada exhausted my capacity for outreach; I didn't think I could ever resume that journey in any form. I no longer wanted to hear your stories, your claims, your grievances. I wanted to shout at your hill: It could have been different! Partner with us, and negotiate a compromise! And *look* at me, acknowledge *my* existence! I've got a story, too.

When I see how my people and its story are portrayed in Palestinian media, I feel close to despair. It seems that the one idea unifying Palestinian media in all its ideological diversity is that the Jews are not a people and have no right to a state. That same message is conveyed in Palestinian schools and mosques. There was no ancient Jewish presence here—that is a Zionist lie. No Temple stood on the Mount. The Holocaust, too, is a Zionist hoax, invented to ensure Western support for Israel. According to the prevailing narrative on your side, I am a pathological liar without any history, a thief without rights to any part of this land, an alien who doesn't belong here.

Israel and the Jews are routinely portrayed in your media as monsters. We were responsible for 9/11, we collaborated with the Nazis in the Holocaust that never happened, we kill Palestinians to harvest their organs, and we even manipulate nature to create environmental disasters. And, of course, we secretly rule the world.

I know Palestinians who are repelled by that demonic portrait of the Jews and who readily acknowledge that we are caught in a conflict between two just narratives. I am hoping you are one of them. But that perspective, from what I see, is banned from your mainstream media. Any voice that even hints at the legitimacy of the Jewish narrative—alongside, not instead of, the Palestinian narrative—is silenced.

How can we ever reconcile if I don't exist, if I have no right to exist?

And so the wall is an expression of a deeper wall between us. We cannot even agree on the most basic shared language. I see my presence here as part of the return of an indigenous, uprooted people, and a reborn Jewish state as an act of historic justice, of reparation. For me, being a Jew in Jerusalem under Israeli sovereignty is a source of uplift, of religious inspiration.

I see your presence in this land as an essential part

of its being. Palestinians often compare themselves to olive trees. I am inspired by your rootedness, by your love for this landscape.

And how do you see me? Am I, in your eyes, part of a colonialist invasion that was a historic crime and a religious violation? Or can you see the Jewish presence here as authentic, just like your own? Can my life here be seen as an uprooted olive tree restored to its place?

As the conflict between us deepens, the wall seems to become more embedded in the landscape, absorbed by the houses and the hills, even by the changing of the light. Often the wall disappears altogether: My eye has learned how not to see. My apartment is high enough for me to look over the wall, to the desert beyond. I can almost evade the constriction and enjoy the expanse.

And yet: The wall remains an insult. A negation of my deepest hope for Israel, which is to find its place among our neighbors.

For years after the second intifada, I said, like most Israelis: We tried to make peace, and we were rebuffed in the most brutal way possible. But that was too easy. As a religious person, I am forbidden to accept this abyss between us as permanent, forbidden to make peace with despair. As the Qur'an so powerfully notes, despair is equivalent to disbelief in God. To doubt the possibility of reconciliation is to limit God's power, the possibility of miracle—especially in this land. The Torah commands me, "Seek peace and pursue it"— even when peace appears impossible, perhaps especially then.

And so I turn to you, neighbor, in the hope that an honest telling of my story may touch you—and help create some understanding, if not agreement, between us. I want my government to actively pursue a two-state solution, explore even the most remote possibility for an agreement. I want my government to speak not only a language of security and threat but also of hope and coexistence and moral responsibility. And I want my government to stop expanding settlements. Not only for your sake, but also for mine. The right-wing Israeli government that exists as I write seems incapable of a visionary approach.

My hope is that now, as we see the devastation in the countries around us—the horrors in Syria and elsewhere in the Middle East—Palestinians and Israelis will together pull back from the abyss, that we will choose life. But for that to happen, we must know each other's dreams and fears.

I went into your society twice—first as a soldier, then as a pilgrim—because I couldn't accept confining my interaction with you to the role of occupier. I will have more to say about that experience. For now I'll say only that I couldn't bear the impact of seemingly endless occupation on the lives of my neighbors—and also on my own moral credibility as a Jew, a carrier of an ancient tradition that cherishes justice and fairness, that places the value of a human life, created in the Divine image, at the core of its worldview.

I am writing these letters as a way of resuming my journey to you. But with this difference: When I last traveled in Palestinian society, I was trying to understand you. For the most part I didn't argue or even speak about myself. Instead I tried to listen.

Now I want to share with you something of my faith and my story, which are entwined. I am a Jew because of history. That is what brought me here, as your neighbor.

Neither of us is likely to convince the other of each side's narrative. Each of us lives within a story so deeply rooted in our being, so defining of our collective and personal existence, that forfeiting our respective narratives would be a betrayal.

But we need to challenge the stories we tell about *each other*, which have taken hold in our societies. We have imposed our worst historical nightmares on the other. To you we are colonialists, Crusaders. And to us you are the latest genocidal enemy seeking to destroy the Jewish people.

Can we, instead, see each other as two traumatized peoples, each clinging to the same sliver of land between the Jordan River and the Mediterranean Sea, neither of whom will find peace or justice until we make our peace with the other's claim to justice?

I don't believe that peace without at least some attempt at mutual understanding can endure. Whatever official document may be signed by our leaders in the future will be undermined on the ground, on your hill and mine. It will be a cold treaty, an unloved peace that will wither and die, or more likely be murdered. If nothing else, the intimacy of our geography makes complete physical separation impossible. And so, to live, we must learn to live together.

True, it's always easier for the victor to be more nuanced, more open to the opposing narrative, than for the conquered. What right do I have as a conqueror to ask you for a reciprocal gesture of recognition? Perhaps because I am a peculiar conqueror: I fear that withdrawal to the nine-mile-wide borders that defined Israel before the 1967 war could fatally undermine my ability to defend myself in a disintegrating Middle East. I fear that withdrawal might not merely diminish but destroy me.

I long ago realized that the historic claims and religious longings that connect me to this land cannot justify my possessing all of it at another people's expense. And so, however painfully, I accept partition as the practical expression of resolving a conflict between two legitimate claims.

But our experience of the widespread rejection of Israel's legitimacy, in Palestinian society and in the Arab and Muslim worlds generally, only hardens us, maddens us. And the refusal to see us as we are—an inseparable part of this region—leads your side to repeatedly underestimate our resolve. No less than you, I am prepared to sacrifice to ensure my place on the land we share.

The key to ending the occupation is giving the Jews some hope that our withdrawal, our willingness to territorially contract, will be reciprocated by a willingness on your side to accept the West Bank and Gaza as the Palestinian state, without trying to undermine the state of Israel.

Perhaps much of what I'm about to write will be hard for you to hear. In the letters that follow, I will be using terms like the "land of Israel," which are a natural part of my vocabulary but may seem to you an affront. That is not my purpose. My hope is that you—someone from your side of the wall—will read this and respond, that you will no longer be an anonymous presence to me but an identity, a voice. Even if you respond in anger. So far whatever has been tried between us has failed miserably and has brought death and destruction to both sides. Let's start talking and see what happens.

And so, neighbor, here I am. I invite you into my spiritual home, in the hope that one day we will be able to welcome each other into our physical homes.

## Need and Longing

Dear Neighbor,

Today is the most terrible day of the Jewish year. It is the fast of Tisha b'Av, the ninth day of the Hebrew month of Av. Compressed into this day of mourning is the destruction of both ancient temples in Jerusalem: the First Temple by the Babylonian king Nebuchadnezzar in 587 BCE, leading to the exile of the Jews to Babylon, and the Second Temple by the Roman general Titus in 70 CE, and the subsequent dispersion of the Jews around the world. The Babylonian exile lasted seventy years, until the Persian king, Cyrus the Great, conquered Babylon and allowed the Jews to return home. The Roman-initiated exile lasted nearly two thousand years, until the creation of the state of Israel in 1948.

As I fast, repeatedly glancing at my watch and waiting for this mini-ordeal to end, I think of Ramadan. The Muslims I know eagerly anticipate those thirty days of fasting as an immersion in sacred time. The thought comforts me, and helps me welcome the spiritual opportunity of self-denial.

The dry heat rising from the desert on this late-July morning feels aptly oppressive. The Hebrew calendar, after all, reflects the natural cycle of this land. We celebrate freedom and renewal on the spring holiday of Passover; we mark the giving of the Torah, the spiritual harvest, on Shavuot at the end of spring, the time of the wheat harvest. And so it's somehow appropriate that the fast of Tisha b'Av occurs during our parched summer, as the land itself seems to convey despair.

Last night I went to the Western Wall, remnant of the Temple left by Tisha b'Av. The stone-paved plaza was crowded with the diversity of the Jews, almost as expansive as humanity itself. Worshippers sat in circles on the ground and read, in the accents of our wanderings, the book of Lamentations—"how the city sits solitary"—composed over twenty-five hundred years ago to mourn the destruction of Jerusalem and our Temple. There were ultra-Orthodox Jews of a dozen sects, distinguished by the sizes and shapes of their black fedoras and by the lengths of their black jackets, chanting in the Yiddish-accented Hebrew of Poland and Hungary. Jews from Yemen with curled side locks chanted in a guttural Hebrew said to resemble the way Jews spoke it before the exile—before Hebrew was confined to liturgy and sacred study, exiled from the nation's vernacular. There was Russian and English and Amharic and especially French: Jews from France are our latest wave of immigrants, fleeing anti-Jewish violence in a Western democracy.

And yet for all the formal gestures of mourning, I didn't sense genuine anguish. Some of the pious cried out the words, but that seemed to me an imitation of grief. It's hard to mourn the exile when the exile has ended.

True, not all Jewish prayers have been answered. We have returned, but the pervasive presence of Israeli soldiers protecting us at the Wall reminds us not only of our restored sovereignty but of continuing threat. Tisha b'Av has been only partly negated. Jewish tradition couldn't imagine this limbo between return and redemption. And so we reenact the choreography of mourning but are restless, disoriented. Home, yet not redeemed.

Moving from circle to circle, I felt a sense of wonder. We have returned to our place of origin, just as Jews always believed would happen, to reconstruct ourselves from disparate communities back into a people.

Most Israelis I know are people of faith—if not necessarily in conventional religion, then surely in a life of meaning. Israelis sense that their very existence—speaking a resurrected language in a recovered homeland—is a miracle. "When the Lord returned the exiles to Zion we were like dreamers," wrote the Psalmist. Being an Israeli is like awakening into a dream.

One morning I was driving my teenage son, Shachar, to school. Not far from the Old City, we got caught in a traffic jam. I said, "You know, in one sense here we are, sitting in a traffic jam, just like in any city anywhere. But sometimes it occurs to me that the most boring details of our daily life were the greatest dreams of our ancestors."

I didn't expect much of a response. Shachar, a jazz musician, tends not to speak in historical categories. But he surprised me. "I think about that a lot," he said.

Of course he does, I realized. How can a Jew live in this country and not think about the improbability of our being?

Once, on a visit to Rome, I went on a pilgrimage of sorts to the Arch of Titus, a monument to the destruction of Jerusalem. On the arch is carved the image of our ruin: Roman legionnaires carrying the Temple menorah through the streets of Rome. During the exile Jews made a point of not walking under the arch, symbolically rejecting submission to defeat. I entered the arch and offered a prayer of gratitude for living in a time when Jewish persistence had been vindicated.

How had the Jews done it? How did our ancestors in exile manage to retain hope? Why for that matter did they stay loyal to their fatally discredited faith, seemingly abandoned by God and superseded by both Christianity and Islam? How did we resist the pressures and temptations to convert to the dominant faiths under which we lived?

Some, of course, did abandon Judaism, which may be one reason why there are so few of us—barely fourteen million. Those who remain Jews are descended from men and women of incomprehensible faith. Our defeated ancestors believed that the story Jews told themselves of exile and return would someday be fulfilled.

One reason I am a believing Jew is because of their faith.

Tisha b'Av presented Judaism with its greatest crisis. Biblical Judaism was centered on the land of Israel and the Temple. But what to do now that a majority of the

Jews had been uprooted from the land and the Temple destroyed?

Gradually Jews realized that, unlike their sojourn in Babylon, this time the exile would be open-ended, with no conclusion in sight. The Jews responded in a paradoxical way. They saw exile as God's punishment for their sins, and so they surrendered to their fate for as long as God decreed. Yet they refused to accept the exile as permanent. They actively nurtured the hope, the faith—the astonishing certainty—that one day the prison sentence of exile would end and God would retrieve them from the most remote corners of the earth, as our prophets had predicted. Still, that prospect was so inconceivable that Jews relegated their return home to the messianic age. Surely only the messiah could restore to sovereignty the most dispersed and powerless among peoples.

In the prolonged interim between Tisha b'Av and redemption, the Jews maintained their dual strategy of accepting exile as a fact and rejecting it as permanent.

The rabbis, popular teachers and arbiters of Jewish law, emerged as the new custodians of Judaism. With the destruction of the Temple, the priests—responsible for its rituals—had become instantly irrelevant. The prophets had been silenced by the withdrawal of Divine revelation, one of the most painful expressions of our spiritual failure. (Prophecy, according to Judaism, is given to Jews only in the land of Israel.) The synagogue became a substitute Temple, prayer a substitute for animal sacrifices—a major step forward in the spiritual evolution of Judaism. Through these innovations, Judaism declared a truce with the exile.

But the rabbis built into the Judaism of exile its own negation, a subversive expectation that one day Tisha b'Av would be reversed—turned into a holiday of redemption. According to Jewish legend, the messiah would be born on Tisha b'Av.

Throughout their wanderings, Jews carried with them the land of Israel, its seasonal rhythms, its stories and prophecies. In their study houses they debated the laws of *shmita*—the commandment to leave the land of Israel fallow every seven years to rest and restore itself. They knew its rhythm of planting and harvesting, as though they were still its farmers. The Jewish relationship to the land of Israel shifted from space to time. For us, the land existed in past and future—memory and anticipation. One day, Jews believed, the land would reemerge from its exile in time, back into space.

Most of all, they preserved the land in prayer. Jewish prayer became suffused with the longing for the land. As a boy, growing up in a religious home in Brooklyn, I prayed in the winter months for rain and in the summer months for dew—regardless of the weather outside my window, following the natural rhythm of a distant land. In morning and evening prayers, in grace after meals, I invoked Zion. Before I'd even known the land of Israel as actual place, I knew it as inherited memory.

When Sarah and I stood under the wedding canopy, we recited, as Jews have done for centuries, the ancient psalm "If I forget you, Jerusalem, let my right hand wither." And then, at the moment of our greatest joy, we broke a glass, in memory of the destroyed Temple.

Perhaps the most powerful expressions of longing for return were contained in the prayer poems of the Jews of Muslim lands. "I will ask my God to redeem the prisoners," Jews sang in Yemen, referring to themselves, exiles from Zion. The medieval Spanish Jewish poet Yehudah Halevi wrote a plaintive prayer adopted by Jews around the world: "Zion, are you not concerned for the well-being of your prisoners?" Moroccan Jews would gather in the synagogue at midnight to sing prayers of return.

In their radically diverse exiles, Jews nurtured rituals of longing—like the holiday of Ethiopian Jews, known as the Sigd. Once a year, in late autumn, thousands of Jews from villages in remote Gondar province would trek up a mountain. Dressed in white, fasting, they turned north toward Zion and prayed for return.

I learned about the Sigd from my friend Shimon, who moved to Israel around the same time I did, in the 1980s. Though he came from the poorest Diaspora community and I came from the most privileged, we had both been raised on the same love of Zion.

For Shimon, the longing to live in Israel began with the Sigd. He proudly informed me that he began fasting at the age of eight.

Severed for centuries from other Jewish communities, Ethiopian Jews believed they were the last Jews in the world. Their Christian neighbors feared them as black magicians—just as Christians in medieval Europe feared Jews as devil-worshippers and well-poisoners—and called them "Falasha," strangers. They called themselves "Beta Yisrael," the House of Israel. And year after year, century after century, they ascended the mountain, their faith mediating between patience and longing.

One day in 1983, Shimon and his family joined their neighbors and began literally walking toward Jerusalem. Israeli rabbis had recently determined that the Beta Yisrael were Jews—a status in dispute because of the community's millennia-long severance from the rest of the Jewish people—and the Israeli government of Prime Minister Menachem Begin let it be known that they were welcome home. And so thousands of Ethiopian Jews were on the move. They walked for weeks through jungle and desert; old people died from exhaustion, children from hunger. No Diaspora community suffered proportionally more fatalities on its way to Zion than the Jews of Ethiopia.

The first stop for Shimon and his family was a refugee camp in the Sudan. Fearful of the Muslim authorities, Shimon and the other Jews concealed their religious identity and waited for Israeli agents to retrieve them. One day a Sudanese soldier, suspecting that Shimon was a Jew, lifted his steel-tipped boot and crushed Shimon's bare foot. He limped ever since.

I think of Ethiopian Jews whenever I hear a Middle Eastern leader say that the only reason Israel exists is the Holocaust, that the Palestinians have paid the price for Western guilt. Many Ethiopian Jews never even heard of the Holocaust until they got to Israel. Half of Israel's Jews come from the Arab world, where, for the most part, the Nazis didn't reach.

Israel exists because it never stopped existing, even if only in prayer. Israel was restored by the cumulative power of Jewish longing. But attachment to the land wasn't confined to longing. Throughout the centuries, Jews from east and west came to live and be buried in the land.

After the Romans destroyed the Judean state, they forbade Jews from living in Jerusalem, a ban reinforced under Christian rule. Muslim rulers of Jerusalem were more gracious. It was, after all, the caliph Umar who, upon conquering Jerusalem in 638 CE, allowed some Jews to return to the city. That kindness is part of the history we share.

The impetus for creating a political expression of the longing for return—restoring the Jewish relationship to Zion from time back into space—was dire need. In nineteenth-century Russia, millions of Jews were threatened by regime-instigated pogroms. Many Russian Jews were fleeing their homes and heading west.

The newly created Zionist movement was seeking a solution not just for Jews but for "the Jews"—a permanent solution to homelessness. Still, however desperate the situation, anti-Semitism and the need for refuge didn't define the essence of Zionism. Need gave Zionism its urgency, but longing gave Zionism its spiritual substance.

Zionism was the meeting point between need and longing.

And when need and longing collided—as they did at a crucial moment in early Zionist history—longing won.

In 1903, the leader of Zionism, Theodor Herzl, a

Viennese journalist obsessed with saving his people, had exhausted his options. Herzl had been an assimilated Jew who came to Zionism because of Jewish need, not longing. But he'd failed to persuade the Turkish sultan to permit mass Jewish immigration into the land of Israel, then a part of the Ottoman Empire. The pope told Herzl that he couldn't support Zionism because Jewish homelessness was Divine punishment for rejecting the messiah. Herzl's movement of impoverished dreamers was virtually bankrupt: Most of the wealthy Jews of Western Europe shunned him, fearing that his plan for a Jewish state would undermine their own efforts to be accepted into gentile society. Good luck with that, Herzl told the Jews of Berlin and Vienna.

Herzl was desperate. The mob violence against Russian Jews was intensifying. Herzl intuited that some unimagined catastrophe, far worse than pogroms, awaited the Jews of Europe.

Then, the British approached him with an offer to settle territory in East Africa. They hoped to get loyal colonists out of Herzl's desire to create a Jewish homeland.

Herzl knew there would be opposition among Zionists to what became known as the Uganda Plan, but the Zionist movement, he believed, was pragmatic. If

Zion was unattainable, he hoped his fellow activists would accept the possible.

Herzl brought the plan before the Zionist Congress. With a map of East Africa hanging behind the podium, he addressed the delegates. Nothing would replace Zion in our hearts, he said. But he urged them to consider the dangers Jews faced, especially in Russia. Need before longing.

He was greeted by cries of anguish. The most vehement opposition came from the young delegates representing Jewish communities in Russia. The very Jews Herzl was trying to save.

A young Russian woman rushed to the podium and ripped the map of Africa off the wall.

The delegates from Russia—led by a young Chaim Weizmann, later Israel's first president—walked out of the hall. They were mostly secular, socialist rebels from religious homes. But their instincts were, at that moment, deeply religious. They gathered in an adjacent room and sat on the floor, the way Jews do in the synagogue on Tisha b'Av. Some of the young people wept. They were in mourning not for Zion but for Zionism.

Herzl went to them. They received the beloved leader, the first Jew in two thousand years to organize a practical way out of exile, with polite coldness. Uganda, Herzl reassured them, would only be a temporary station on the way to Zion. Herzl managed to prevent a schism in the Zionist movement, but the Russian delegates remained deeply opposed.

In his closing speech to the Congress, Herzl raised his right hand and repeated the words of the Psalms, "If I forget you, Jerusalem, let my right hand wither."

A year later, Herzl died—at age forty-four, of exhaustion and heart failure. His rescue mission had faltered. Catastrophe would not be averted.

After the Uganda Plan, there were other attempts to create Jewish "homelands" in various parts of the world—like Birobidzhan, the Soviet fantasy of a Yiddish-speaking Communist homeland on the Chinese border. But every alternative to Zion failed.

Had the Uganda Plan prevailed, Zionism would have become a frankly colonialist movement. A tragic colonialism, impelled not by greed or glory but existential need. Still, there would be no escaping that hard judgment against Zionism.

But by insisting on Zion—against all odds, no matter the consequences—Zionism affirmed its legitimacy as a movement of repatriation, restoring a native people home.

Precisely because Zionism is such a unique phenomenon, it is tempting to fit it into other categories, like nineteenth-century European nationalism. From there it is a small step to defining Zionism as a colonialist movement.

Zionism was of course strongly influenced by European nationalism. But that was only the form that a two-thousand-year dream of return assumed. And though launched in the West, Zionism reached its culmination in the East. When the state of Israel was established, whole Jewish communities in the Middle East moved to Zion.

The first community to answer the call were the Jews of Yemen. Throughout 1949, an ancient community of over 40,000 was flown home in Israel's first airlift. Many Yemenite Jews, who had never seen a plane, recalled the biblical promise to restore the Jews from exile "on the wings of eagles" and assumed that that prophecy was being literally fulfilled on the tarmac.

Then, in 1951, came the turn of the ancient Jewish community of Iraq. Over a hundred thousand Iraqi Jews—virtually the entire community—were flown to Israel, the largest airlift in history. They included cosmopolitan Jews of Baghdad and village Jews of Kurdistan, mystics and Communists and Zionist activists.

And then came the Jews of North Africa. And Egypt. And Syria. And Lebanon. One ancient Jewish community after another emptying into the state of Israel.

A majority of Israelis today are descended from Jews who left one part of the Middle East to resettle in another. Tell them that Zionism is a European colonialist movement and they simply won't understand what you're talking about.

Jews from the East were present at the very beginning of the political return to Zion. In 1882, Yemenite kabbalists calculated that the Hebrew equivalent of that date would be the year of redemption. And so several hundred Yemenite Jews set sail for Jaffa harbor, expecting to greet the messiah.

Instead they encountered the first group of Zionist pioneers from Russia. It was not a joyful reunion of brothers. The two groups of Jews from either end of the Diaspora regarded each other warily. The misunderstandings only grew between the deeply traditionalist Jews of the East and the brash young pioneers from Europe.

And yet the Yemenite kabbalists were, in a sense, right: The year 1882 was one of redemption for the Jews, because it marked the beginning of the modern return to Zion. And there, at the moment of birth, was a meeting, however difficult, between the Jewish East and the Jewish West. There had been no prior com-

munication between them; the Jews of Yemen didn't
know about the groups of young Zionists forming in
Europe.

Those Yemenites weren't "Zionists" in any political sense. But they were Zionists in the deepest sense:
They were Jews returning to their homeland, in anticipation of the restoration of their people's sovereignty.

Zionism came full circle by the end of the twentieth century, with the mass immigration to Israel of
Russian Jews, refugees from seventy years of Communism. Subjected to government-imposed assimilation, forbidden to study and practice their faith, many
hardly seemed Jewish at all. But here they have rejoined the Jewish people, learning Hebrew and living
by the rhythms of the Jewish calendar and marrying
Jews from other parts of the Diaspora. Israel is the one
place where assimilation works in favor of Jewish continuity.

I have heard Palestinian leaders cite the immigration from Russia—with its large numbers of inter-
married couples—as proof of the inauthentic nature
of Jewish nationhood. From a Zionist perspective,
though, none of our waves of immigration is more or
less "authentic." Traditional Jews from Iraq and Yemen, assimilated Jews from the former Soviet Union:
All are indigenous sons and daughters returning home.

Is it possible, as anti-Zionists insist, to separate Zionism from Judaism? Is Zionism mere "politics," as opposed to Judaism, which is authentic "religion"?

The answer depends on what one means by Zionism. If it refers to the political movement that emerged in the late nineteenth century, then certainly, there are forms of Judaism that are independent of Zionism. In the era before the establishment of Israel, Jews vehemently debated the wisdom of the Zionist program. Marxist Jews rejected Zionism as a diversion from the anticipated world revolution. Ultra-Orthodox Jews rejected Zionism as a secularizing movement, while some insisted that only the messiah could bring the Jews home.

But if by "Zionism" one means the Jewish attachment to the land of Israel and the dream of renewing Jewish sovereignty in our place of origin, then there is no Judaism without Zionism. Judaism isn't only a set of rituals and rules but a vision linked to a place. Modern movements that created forms of Judaism severed from the love of the land and the dream of return all ended in failure.

By the time the state was established, anti-Zionism had become peripheral in Jewish life. Aside from a vocal fringe, most ultra-Orthodox Jews made their peace with a Jewish state. Israel's Declaration of Independence was signed by representatives of almost the entire spectrum of the Jewish community—from ultra-Orthodox to Communists. That document attests to the legitimacy, within the Jewish people, of the state created by Zionism.

In recent years there have been renewed attempts, especially on the fringes of the Diaspora left, to create a Jewish identity severed from Israel. But with nearly half the world's Jews living in a thriving Jewish-majority state, that debate has long since been resolved. If in the past one couldn't separate the land of Israel from Jewish life, today the same holds true for the state of Israel.

In the summer of 1982, shortly after Tisha b'Av, I left my home in New York City, boarded an El Al plane, and joined the Jewish people in the greatest dare of its history. I was twenty-nine years old, a journalist, and single. I left my old life behind, without looking back.

The Lebanon War had just begun, and Israel was bitterly divided. Left-wingers and right-wingers shouted at each other in the streets. Inflation was running at 300 percent. And I was home.

In a way, it was good to come at such a low point in Israel's history. It left little room for illusion and disappointment. I came without preconditions and expectations. However this story played out, it would now be my story.

When people "back home" were puzzled and asked me why I'd left America for the Middle East, I used a journalistic metaphor: I needed to know Israeli reality not only from the headlines but from the back pages. I wanted to know the texture, the nuances of the Jewish return.

Everything seemed at once familiar and strange. I walked the streets slowly, feeling like a time traveler who had stumbled into the Jewish future. So this is what it looked like when the Jews returned home, I repeated to myself.

I felt humbled by the fortitude that ordinary Israelis take for granted, their capacity to contend with war and terror and wave after wave of destitute immigrants. I felt privileged to be living the Jewish holidays in the place where they were meant to be observed. I laughed at the absurdities of Israeli life of the early 1980s, like the television tax I paid for the pleasure of watching the single black-and-white government-run TV station. I tried to understand the emotional and psychological impact of life in a pressure cooker. Why did you leave America, you didn't have it good there? perplexed Israeli teenagers asked me, and then inquired how they could get an American visa.

Through it all, one constant anxiety has accompanied me: Are the Jews going to make it this time? After all, we lost this land twice before. The great irony of Jewish history is that, for all the centrality in Judaism of the land of Israel, we've lived far more of our history outside of it than in it. We are a people of both homeland and Diaspora. The Torah warns us that the land "will vomit you out"—the language could hardly be more explicit—if we don't live up to God's expectations. In the words of one Jewish prayer, "We were exiled from our land because of our sins." A terrifying conditionality haunts our return. Jewish sovereignty has been entrusted to us; will we be the generation on whose watch it unravels?

The challenges facing us are overwhelming. How to refashion a single people out of scattered communities that had little communication for centuries? How to balance religious and secular identities? How to create a shared civic space between Jewish Israelis and Arab Israelis? How to make peace with enemies who don't accept our right to be here? How to defend ourselves against threat from every border? How to empower your people without endangering my people?

The consolation Israelis draw is that the challenges we've faced have been nearly impossible from the very beginning of our return. Israel has constantly surprised itself—in good ways and bad. It sometimes seems that we are intent on compensating for two millennia of lost sovereignty by cramming into mere decades the fulfillment of all our dreams, while repeating all the mistakes that other nations commit over centuries.

Yet none of Israel's dilemmas or failures has ever caused me to regret my decision to live here. The opposite: Israel's flaws are challenges, not deterrents. They are *my* flaws, distortions in my own Jewish being that I need to confront. In success or failure, in glory or disgrace: The fate of Israel is my fate, too, my shared responsibility. That, for me, is the meaning of Zionism.

Judaism was intended to be lived communally, shaping a society's ethics and behavior. Here, then, is our chance to test our most noble ideas—abstractions in exile—against hard reality. This is where the worthiness of the Jewish story is being decided.

Though moving here was an individual decision, I was accepted by Israel as part of a people returning home. It didn't matter if I'd come from New York or Mumbai, if I would be an economic asset or a burden. I was a Jew returning home, and so eligible for Israeli citizenship.

I was admitted under the "Law of Return," which grants citizenship to any Jew requesting it. I imagine that the first law that the state of Palestine will pass will be your own law of return, granting automatic citizenship to any Palestinian in your diaspora who wants to come home. That is the duty of a state whose existence is meant to undo exile.

Every time I land at Ben-Gurion Airport after a trip abroad, and head for the line earmarked for Israeli passport holders, I experience something of the thrill I felt as a new immigrant. I tell myself to stop being sentimental, but it doesn't work. After all these years, I'm still grateful to be an Israeli returning home.

For all the idealistic and aspirational motives that brought me to Israel, in the end I came for one reason: because it was possible. I was privileged to live in the time when Tisha b'Av was no longer the defining judgment on Jewish history.

# Fate and Destiny

Dear Neighbor,

So who are the Jews? A religion? A people? An ethnicity? A race?

That question impacts directly on our conflict. It goes to the heart of the Arab world's rejection of Israel's legitimacy as the nation-state of the Jewish people.

The Jews began as a family. Four thousand years ago, Abraham and Sarah founded a dynasty that became a people and a faith. But family—a basic sense of belonging to a community of fate, regardless of your religious or political beliefs—has remained at the core of Jewish identity ever since.

Family ties among Jews can be expressed in dramatic ways. My formative experience of belonging to a global Jewish family was the protest movement to save the Jews of the former Soviet Union. I joined that movement in the 1960s, as a boy in Brooklyn, protesting for Jews I never met living thousands of miles away. But family knows no borders: It was self-evident to me that if my brothers and sisters were in crisis, my responsibility was to help save them. By "saving" Soviet Jewry, we didn't mean protecting them from physical danger, because they weren't threatened with actual destruction. But their Jewish identity was under assault by a government policy that banned Jewish education and practice, that was attempting to erase them as Jews. And so we set out to prevent losing them as part of the family.

Jews around the world organized a sustained campaign of protests that lasted for twenty-five years and helped redefine Jewish identity and purpose. Thousands of Jews from around the Diaspora traveled to the Soviet Union, simply to meet with fellow Jews and encourage them to persist. The protest campaign spread around the world, until almost every Jewish community, no matter how small or remote, was drawn into the effort. Finally, the gates of the Soviet Union opened in the late 1980s and the lost Jews rejoined their people.

The Jewish family also manifests in more intimate ways. In my travels, I've experienced the blessings of belonging to an extended and generous family, expanding my sense of home. In Mumbai I was hosted by a childless Jewish couple and treated as a son, because in a sense I was. While spending a year in a village in southern France, I was astonished one day to receive boxes of fresh produce, a gift for the Jewish new year from someone I didn't know: a farmer who'd heard that a fellow Jew was visiting from abroad. "Are you a Jew?" I'm sometimes asked in airports, and it's not hard to tell whether the question is being asked with hostility or anticipation.

Adversity has diminished us but also made us stronger. One reason Jews care so passionately about each other is because of historical necessity. That sense of family has impacted our conflict, too, neighbor. Every attempt to destroy or undermine Israel over the years only strengthened the support for the Jewish state from Jews around the world.

But, paradoxically, this overwhelming sense of family can also undermine Jewish solidarity. As in any family, mutual expectations can lead to feelings of betrayal. When Jews determine that fellow family members have betrayed either the interests or the values of the community, they can turn against each other with a ferocious contempt. That is the dark side of Jewish family.

The form that Jewish family takes is peoplehood.

The centrality of peoplehood in Jewish identity helps explain the seeming anomaly of Jewish atheists. In Islam and Christianity, for example, adherents who stop believing in the basic tenets of the faith are no longer Muslims or Christians. But Jews without faith, who still remain faithful to their people—contributing to its well-being, raising their children as Jews—will be widely regarded by fellow Jews as within the fold.

Over the years I have repeatedly heard variations of the following from Palestinians, and from Muslims generally: We have no problem with the Jews as a religion. We treated you better than the Christians did. But we have no sympathy for your insistence that you are a people, with the right to national sovereignty, because we know you aren't a people but a religion.

The denial of Jewish peoplehood is one of the key divides between us. Even Palestinian moderates I've known who want to end the bloodshed tend to deny that the Jews are an authentic nation. So long as Palestinian leaders insist on defining the Jews as a religion rather than allowing us to define ourselves as we have since ancient times—as a people with a particular faith—then Israel will continue to be seen as illegitimate, its existence an open question.

For Judaism, peoplehood has a crucial spiritual dimension. If the Jews were just a family whose concern was self-preservation—a family bound only by shared fate—then it's doubtful we would have survived through thousands of years of wandering and adversity. The Jewish collective functions on two levels: as family and as faith. What strengthened the Jewish family was its sense of destiny—that the Jewish people has an urgent spiritual role to play in the evolution of humanity. Destiny gives meaning to fate.

Judaism is the love story between God and a people. That romance is often tumultuous. Sometimes, as the Bible records, God accuses the Jews of faithlessness, and sometimes Jews reciprocate and accuse God of abandoning the covenant with them, especially in times of acute persecution. But so long as the Jewish people exist, the love story persists.

The purpose of Judaism is to sanctify one people with the goal of sanctifying all peoples. According to this belief, God set aside a random group of human beings—emphatically not a nation of saints—and exposed them to mass revelation at Mount Sinai, where God appeared not only to Moses, a single great soul, but to all of Israel. The very ordinariness of the people of Israel—a nation of freed slaves—was in some sense the point of their chosenness. The Jews were chosen, in other words, not because they were innately special but because they weren't: the national equivalent of "everyman"—every people, any people. They were to be a test case for what happens when a cross-section of humanity is subjected to an unmediated encounter with the Divine. Sinai was a rehearsal for the revelation that humanity will experience at the culmination of history.

For all the beliefs and values Jews share with Muslims and Christians as fellow monotheists, there is a crucial distinction. Islam and Christianity are universal faiths, intended in principle for every human being. Each of these faiths envisions a future world that will be remade in its image; each believes that, at the end of history, humanity will embrace its way.

Judaism, by contrast, is a faith intended for a specific people.

Judaism shares with Islam and Christianity a universal vision: that the reality of God will one day be as self-evident as material reality is today. All three faiths aim at preparing humanity for the revelation of God's presence. In the Jewish dream of the future, all of humanity will recognize the unity of existence and ascend on pilgrimage to the "house of God" in Jerusalem.

But Judaism has no expectation that humanity will

become Jewish. Instead, the role of the Jews is to be a spiritual avant-garde, attesting to God's presence—not least through their improbable survival—and helping prepare humanity for its breakthrough to transcendence: a particularist strategy for a universal goal.

The structure of the Hebrew Bible reveals the purpose of the Jews. It begins as a universal story: the creation of the first humans; their mysterious fall into this physical world from the "Garden of Eden," a higher state of being; the beginning of fratricide; the inability of humanity to transcend the level of animal existence—culminating in an apocalyptic destruction the Bible calls "the flood."

The failure of humanity to fulfill God's plan required a new Divine strategy. And so God appointed Abraham to found a people, through whom, as the Bible puts it, "all the nations of the earth will be blessed." The Bible then narrowed its focus and became the story of a people, struggling to rise above human nature and become "a kingdom of priests and a holy nation." God's redemptive plan for humanity required a people to carry that vision through history. For Judaism, then, peoplehood and faith are inseparable. There is no Judaism without a Jewish people.

The Hebrew Bible culminates with a universal vision—a time when the presence of God will be, in

Isaiah's words, "as visible as the waters of the sea" and humanity will embrace its oneness. The biblical narrative returns to its universal roots and humanity returns to the Garden, but at a higher evolutionary state, having matured through its experiences in history.

Each religious strategy—the universal approach of Islam and Christianity, and the peoplehood approach of Judaism—has a spiritual advantage and disadvantage. The advantage of a universal faith is that it sees all of humanity as its immediate responsibility. I am deeply moved by the scenes of millions of pilgrims gathering in Mecca, representing a multiplicity of nations. Yet all-embracing universal faiths must struggle against the temptation to define their path as the only legitimate way to God.

Because Judaism is intended for a specific people, it can accommodate the validity of other faiths. As a Jew, I have no expectations of remaking humanity in my religious image, and so I feel grateful to other faiths for offering varied paths to God. Islam and Christianity have brought vast numbers of souls into a relationship with God—and, as it happens, with the sacred stories of my people. Now Judaism is encountering Hinduism and Buddhism, and rabbis and scholars are beginning to grapple with a Jewish understanding of those essential faiths.

The danger of a peoplehood-based faith is self-obsession. There is a tendency, especially among the most fervently traditional Jews, to ignore the rest of humanity and its problems. Partly that's a consequence of thousands of years of persecution, which have driven many Jews into a kind of protective insularity. Still, the temptation facing Judaism is to forget its universal goal and imagine that God's overriding concern isn't humanity but a single people.

The Jews are not a hermetically closed people, let alone an ethnicity or a race—as any street scene in Israel, with its radical human diversity, will reveal. Judaism is open to converts. Orthodox Judaism makes the conversion process arduous (other Jewish denominations less so). But once completed, a convert is regarded as any other Jew. Fellow Jews are forbidden to remind converts of their origins, to avoid conveying, even subtly, the message of exclusion from the community of Israel.

One of the most beloved Jewish figures is Ruth the Moabite, who converted to Judaism and is the great-grandmother of King David, founder of the messianic line. The tradition linking a convert to the messiah is a reminder to Jews: We are a particular people with a universal goal.

According to the book of Ruth, the conversion process of King David's great-grandmother consisted simply of a declaration. Ruth told her Israelite mother-in-law, Naomi: "Your people will be my people, your God my God."

The order of those two vows reveals something essential about how ancient Judaism viewed not only the process of becoming a Jew but the nature of Jewish identity. First Ruth declares her allegiance to the people of Israel. And then she affirms her faith in God. The foundation of Jewishness is peoplehood.

One argument I've heard from some Palestinians is that the state of Israel lacks historical legitimacy because Ashkenazim—Jews of European origin—aren't descended from the ancient Israelites at all but from the medieval Khazars—a Turkic tribe whose king, along with many of his people, converted to Judaism in the eighth century CE. The notion that Ashkenazi Jews are descended from the Khazars is dismissed by most historians. (And what of the Mizrahim—Jews of Middle Eastern origin?)

But even if all Jews alive today were descended from the Khazars, it wouldn't affect their legitimacy as Jews. Converts and born Jews are interchangeable; once you commit to the Jewish people and its faith, you are retroactively linked to its very origins—to the first Jewish converts, Abraham and Sarah. There is even the mystical notion that the souls of converts stood at Mount Sinai to receive the Torah along with the rest of the Jewish people.

My wife, Sarah, who grew up Christian, experienced a conversion process similar to Ruth's. First she fell in love with the Jewish people (like Ruth, through a particular Jew), and then she came to love the God of the Jewish people and take on its path. When she converted she chose the name Sarah because, like her biblical namesake, she, too, was founding a Jewish line.

Having been formed for a Divine purpose, the Jewish people itself became a religious category. Loyalty to the Jewish people is, for Judaism, a *religious* act. That's why religious Zionists never hesitated to partner with secular Zionists, who love and protect their people. For religious Jews, strengthening the Jewish people contributes to its ability to function as a Divine messenger in the world.

The inherent relationship between peoplehood and religion hasn't always been accepted by every Jewish group. In the nineteenth century, for example, Reform Judaism declared the Jews to be only a faith. That position has since evolved, and today Reform Judaism embraces a normative Jewish identity that includes peoplehood and attachment to Israel. On the opposite end of the religious spectrum are the ultra-Orthodox, who emerged in nineteenth-century Europe as an antimodernist ideology and whose relationship to peoplehood is ambivalent. While surely accepting peoplehood as part of their religious identity, the separatist ultra-Orthodox in effect place stringent religious practice ahead of basic Jewish unity, alienating much of the mainstream Jewish community.

The notion of a people chosen by God wasn't intended to bestow privilege but responsibility. Jewish history attests that this role carries more burden than glory. The classical way Jews understood their own history was as the story of a people failing to live in the intensity of God's presence. This is the story told by the Hebrew Bible—a national epic astonishing in its relentless criticism of the people it is supposedly intended to celebrate.

With the rise of Christianity and Islam, the Jewish self-critique of our spiritual failures became an external assault on our very legitimacy. Judaism was dismissed as obsolete, a failure. But Jews resisted that judgment. Living for centuries in often hostile lands, they still believed that God intended them to play a key spiritual role in history. And that role would be activated once they returned home, where they would function again as a sovereign collective.

There are Jews who distort chosenness, transforming it from a basis for serving humanity into an aggrieved separatism from the world. Chosenness can become a form of conceit, a self-glorifying theology. One can readily find examples of chauvinism, along with the opposite, in the vast corpus of Jewish religious literature. For some Jews, particularism becomes an end in itself, and the very universal purpose for which the people of Israel was appointed—to be a blessing for the nations—is displaced by an exaggerated sense of Jewish centrality.

But we also face the opposite problem.

Throughout our history there have been Jews who, longing for the universal endpoint, opted out of the Jewish people altogether. If the goal is human oneness, why continue clinging to an outmoded separatism? That, in effect, was the argument of Saul of Tarsus, who became Saint Paul. An impatience with "tribalism" led many Jews in the nineteenth and twentieth centuries to exchange Jewish identity for messianic Marxism, with disastrous consequences, not least for the Jews themselves.

Sustaining the tension between the particular and the universal is one of the great challenges facing the Jewish people today. One part has barricaded itself within the most constricted and triumphalist aspects of our tradition, while another part is so open to the rest of the world that it risks fading out of the Jewish story altogether.

For me, carrying a four-thousand-year tradition that has thrived despite sometimes overwhelming hostility is a privilege and a responsibility. Our story has been a vital part of the human story, and I believe that humanity still needs the voice of Jewish history. In my Jewish identity, the particular and the universal coexist. One commitment reinforces the other.

# Narrative and Presence

Dear Neighbor,

Today is Israel's Independence Day, and my hill is covered in the national colors of blue and white. There are small Israeli flags flying from car windows—some cars boast two flags—and larger ones hanging from balconies.

So much history has been condensed into these seven decades of independence. We leaped from pioneering Israel where young people worked the land with a kind of religious devotion, to postmodern Israel with shopping malls and reality TV. From an impoverished agrarian backwater to an economic power with one of the world's largest numbers of high-tech start-ups. From shantytowns crowded with Jewish refugees to Tel Aviv's glass towers. From the most egalitarian society among Western-style countries, with the smallest wage differential between the prime minister and the person who cleaned his office, to a society with one of the West's greatest wage disparities. From admired little Israel of the communal kibbutz to reviled "greater Israel" of the West Bank settlements.

Israel's greatest success is its population: nearly nine million citizens, close to two million of them Arabs. Israel contains the largest Jewish community—almost half of the world's Jews. If present demographic trends continue, a majority of the world's Jews will soon live here. When the state was founded in 1948, there were half a million.

A helicopter crosses your hill. I feel an involuntary relief: We are being protected, especially on this day, a tempting time for terror attacks. But then I think of you: How frightening it must be for you and your children to hear helicopters hovering over your home. This is the curse of our relationship: My protection is your vulnerability, my celebration your defeat.

The inverse can also be true. Sometimes my misfortune evokes joy among some of my Palestinian neighbors. When missiles are launched by Hezbollah on Israeli towns in the north, or by Hamas on towns in the south, celebratory fireworks light up your hill.

Sarah and I invited family and friends over for the holiday and we picnic on the grass outside our apartment. We watch the same old Israeli comedies on TV that we watch every Independence Day. We feel no pull to go anywhere; this is a day for the simple pleasures of home.

Yesterday, Memorial Day for our fallen soldiers, we grieved. That Independence Day follows the very next day is an expression of our emotionally polarized national life. And yet there is also something profound about this intimacy of mourning and celebration, the insistence on remembering the price we paid for independence. The saddest moment in this country is not Holocaust Day, which we observed last week, but Memorial Day, a reminder that this is a country where parents sometimes must bury their children so that Israel can live. On Holocaust Day, we mourn the consequences of powerlessness; on Memorial Day, we mourn the consequences of power.

The near-total absence of nationalist bombast on Memorial Day is extraordinary for a country under permanent siege. The songs on the radio are mournful, quiet; the short films on TV, each focusing on a young life taken too soon, tell human stories more than national ones. There is deep love of country in these short documentaries, but no glorification of sacrifice.

The young men are sometimes remembered as heroes, but always as sons, brothers, friends. When a soldier falls, we turn him back into a child.

There is, of course, another anniversary that will follow our Independence Day: your day of mourning, Nakba Day. The Palestinian catastrophe of 1948. Not of 1967, not of the occupation and the West Bank settlements, but of the founding of Israel. That is the heart of the Palestinian grievance against me. My national existence.

And so, neighbor, before we discuss how to reach a two-state solution based on the 1967 borders, we need to go back to 1948—and even earlier, to the origins of the conflict. Back to 1882, when the first group of young Zionists landed in Jaffa harbor. We need to understand the competing historic narratives that we carry with us and that the diplomats have tried to bypass on their way to a solution—not surprisingly, with such dismal results.

I have before me a book of photographs of the Holy Land. The photos were commissioned by the late-nineteenth-century Turkish sultan Abdul Hamid II, and portray the land in the moment before the Zionists appeared. There are photographs of holy places, caught in seeming timelessness, without the crowds of worshippers and tourists that gather there today. The villages and even towns appear sparse, overwhelmed by empty surroundings.

The photographs I keep returning to are those of the Arabs. Here is a group of women gathered near a well, pitchers on heads; a man and a woman sit facing each other on boulders, speaking without self-consciousness before the camera; a white-bearded sheikh in turban and robes smiles into the distance.

By contrast, the Jews in this album seem beaten by circumstance. They are the pious residents of the "old *yishuv*," the Jewish community that predated the Zionist immigration and existed in the land for centuries as a minority. In these images there are no smiles, no easy gestures. The bearded men, some with stained caftans, appear to be enduring a bitter old age. Almost everyone in this album, Arab and Jew, is poor, yet the poverty of the Jews seems more ravaging. There is no sign of normal life, no Jewish goatherds or plowmen. Instead the men are photographed either praying or simply posing with religious books. (Jewish women are nowhere to be seen.) Some had come to die in the Holy Land; most lived on donations from Jews abroad.

I'm grateful to those Jews of the old *yishuv* for keeping alive the organic connection of the people of Israel with Zion. Their very presence here was a reminder

of the promise of eventual return. And yet I understand the contempt that the first Zionists felt toward
them. The young pioneers had left behind the ghettos
of Europe to build a new Jewish life of working the
land—only to encounter, in the old Jewish quarters of
Jerusalem and Hebron and Safed, the same bent backs
of the ghetto, the conditioned wariness, the poverty of
passivity. The old *yishuv* embodied the corrosive effect
of exile on Jewish life: even those Jews living in the
land of Israel seemed uprooted.

The final photograph of the album shows the boatmen of Jaffa harbor who transported passengers and
cargo from arriving ships, which couldn't dock because of boulders. A crew of nine men, some in fezzes,
sit in a long boat, oars up and ready; in the distance
two ships approach. I imagine young Jewish pioneers
on those ships, straining to catch a glimpse of their
new home. In a moment the boatmen will be galvanized, and they will transport the immigrants into the
harbor.

I want to linger on this photograph. Not for its ar-
tistic quality: The faces aren't clear and the photograph
is banal. Yet for me this is the book's most poignant
image, precisely because its protagonists have no idea
that they are presiding over the moment of transition
that will shatter their world forever.

The young Zionists arrived with a powerful narrative—a four-thousand-year story that linked their people to this land. They came to be builders and plowmen and goatherds—the opposite of the Jews of Sultan Abdul Hamid's photographs. Their success was to reindigenize the Jewish people, raising one generation after another of Jewish natives in this land.

I've often heard from Palestinians that, just as the Ottoman Turks came here and left, and the British came here and left, so, too, will the Zionists one day leave. That analogy ignores Zionism's singular achievement. None of those invaders founded a thriving society, let alone a sovereign state. They eventually went back to their own homelands. More than anything else, I need you to understand this: The Jews succeeded where the Crusaders and the Ottomans and the British failed because we didn't merely come here. We returned.

Tragically, each side has tried, at different stages of the conflict, to deny the legitimacy of the other's national identity, to rationalize the other out of existence. Some Jews continue to try to "prove" that Palestinian national identity is a fiction, that you are a contrived people. Of course you are—and so are we. All national identities are, by definition, contrived: At a certain point, groups of people determine that they share more in common than apart and invent themselves as a nation, with a common language, memory, and evolving story. The emergence of a nation is an inherently subjective process. As an old Hebrew song about the birth of modern Zionism put it, "Suddenly a person wakes up in the morning / feels himself to be a nation / and starts walking." I know of no better description for the creation of a people.

We need to respect each other's right to tell our own stories. That's why I am writing to you, neighbor: to tell you my story, not yours. If you choose to write in response, as I hope you will, you'll tell me your understanding of your history. I respect your right to define yourself, and I insist on the same right. That is the way to peace.

I came to understand something of the power of Palestinian national identity while serving as a soldier in the time of the first intifada. Patrolling in Gaza and the West Bank, I confronted young people throwing rocks against soldiers with guns, fighting for their people, and felt respect for them as worthy adversaries. In their place I would have done the same. The first intifada was the moment when many Israelis began to realize that we'd been wrong to dismiss Palestinian nationhood. An Israeli majority gradually coalesced around the two-state solution—until then a position held in Israel mostly by a Far Left fringe. The Palestinian right to self-determination became a part of mainstream Israeli discourse.

Yet the Palestinian national movement, from Fatah to Hamas, along with much of the Arab and Muslim worlds, continues to dismiss the very notion of a Jewish people. Initially, that denial was understandable. Jews, after all, had lived for centuries under Islam as a religious minority. Why, Muslims argued, should we accept the nineteenth-century reinvention of the Jews as a nation? That perception was based on a fundamental misreading of how Jews always understood themselves: as a people with a particular faith. Jews lived as a religious minority by the coercion of circumstance; they never stopped anticipating the moment when they would be transformed back into a sovereign nation. That hope was a foundation of their religious faith.

When the conflict began, this land was largely empty. That is the overwhelming impression conveyed by the photographs of Sultan Abdul Hamid, and statistics confirm it. In the late nineteenth century, there were barely half a million residents—the overwhelming majority Arabs. (Today nearly thirteen million people, Israelis and Palestinians, live between the river and the sea.) Even as the presence of both Arab and Jewish communities grew, the land was able to accommodate two nations.

Zionism's intention was to resettle the Jews, not dispossess the Palestinians. Even the most maximalist Zionist leader of the pre-state era, Ze'ev Jabotinsky, accepted as self-evident that the future Jewish state would include a large Arab minority, which, he wrote, would be granted equality with Jews.

Was the clash between our peoples inevitable?

Given each side's narrative and needs, coexistence was, in retrospect, likely impossible. In the 1930s, Zionist and Palestinian leaders quietly tried to reach a compromise. But while the mainstream Zionist position in those years supported two states for two peoples, the mainstream Palestinian position rejected any Jewish sovereignty on any part of the land, no matter how small.

The conflict focused largely on Jewish immigration. The Jews needed to reconstitute themselves as a sovereign majority in at least part of the land, which meant bringing in large numbers of immigrants; while the Palestinians sought to prevent themselves from being turned into a minority in any part of the land, which meant trying to block Jewish immigration.

Another clash of basic interests emerged over "Hebrew labor"—the socialist Zionist ethos of encouraging young Jews to adopt a life of manual work. In those years, the Zionist mainstream was largely socialist, with a strong radical left wing. According to the old socialist Zionist ideology, Jewish life in the exile had been corrupted in several ways, especially economically. Through the centuries Jews had often been forbidden to own land and become farmers, and so they were forced onto the economic margins. For socialist Zionists, healing the Jewish people meant transforming Jews from traders and luftmensch intellectuals into a peasant and working class. The only way to build a self-sufficient Jewish society in the land of Israel, socialist Zionists argued, was to create a Jewish proletariat—avoiding at all costs a stratified society in which Jews were the managers and Arabs the workers.

But when the socialist pioneers began to arrive around the turn of the twentieth century, they encountered, to their horror and shame, a very different reality. The non-socialist pioneers who had preceded them in the first Zionist wave that began in 1882 had established agricultural villages in which Arab peasants were employed as cheap labor. Here was the socialists' worst nightmare. How could a Jewish state be built by a landed class? For socialists, the very future of the Jewish people depended on creating a Jewish working class. And so the young pioneers organized themselves into a union and competed with Arabs for field hand jobs. The purpose wasn't to deny Arabs work but to get Jews to work. The result was the emergence of a Jewish working class—sometimes at the expense of Arab workers.

"Hebrew labor" is instructive because it reveals the impossible choices facing Zionism. Opt for the non-socialist way and you end up ruling over Arab workers; opt for the socialist way and you turn the job market into a struggle between two peoples.

The greatest source of conflict between our peoples was over land. First under Ottoman rule, then under British rule, the Zionist movement bought tracts of land—and every *dunam* settled by Jews during these decades was paid for. In this decisive phase of re-planting an active Jewish presence, there was no land confiscation. The Zionist movement bought land from whoever was legally entitled to sell. That often meant absentee Arab landlords. Sometimes the land was uninhabited—malaria-infested marshes or rocky terrain—for which the Zionists paid exorbitant prices. (Land prices increased by *5,000 percent* between 1910 and 1944, mainly because of Zionist purchases.) But the stubborn Jews turned the seemingly least inhabit-able terrain into fields and gardens.

Some of these lands owned by absentee landlords

were inhabited by Arab peasants who'd worked them for their entire lives and who were now evicted, though with some financial compensation. That it was often radical socialists creating egalitarian communes on the newly purchased land only deepened the irony. One more piece of an unfolding tragedy, in which neither side could avoid seeing the other as an obstacle to its most basic needs.

As I contemplate this history, one part of me cheers and another is deeply saddened. I cheer the heroic young people, barely out of their teens, sacrificing their best years to plant and till, to prepare the land for the Jewish return. And I mourn for your people, neighbor, for the people in the sultan's photographs whose lives are gradually disrupted and, as the conflict between our sides reaches its seminal moment in 1948, uprooted and destroyed. And I mourn, dear neighbor, for you and for me, because, just as the opportunity for a two-state solution was squandered in 1947, we, too, seem caught in the contradictory logic of an existential conflict, to which each generation adds its own measure of bitterness and mutual grievance.

There are times I can't bear anymore this disputation between us. Any argument that either of us can offer—over history, ideology, politics—seems to contain its counterargument. How much energy have we wasted trying to prove the justness of our claims and the supposed hollowness of the other's claims? How much of the world's attention has been diverted to this seemingly endless sparring? An Armenian acquaintance, a historian, once told me how unbearable it was for him to squander his time writing about his people's genocide, refuting Turkish denials. It's humiliating, he said, intellectually stifling. How many unwritten books, he lamented, has he sacrificed to Armenian polemics?

I, too, feel depleted by this argument between us. But I continue because the legitimacy of Israel's story is under assault, and this threatens the heart of Jewish existence. My definition for the Jews is this: We are a story we tell ourselves about who we think we are. That's why the central Jewish ritual that most Jews continue to observe, no matter how far removed from Judaism, is the Passover seder, the retelling of our ancient origins as a people.

I hope a time will come when we no longer feel the need to argue over our shared traumatic past and will instead be focused on our shared future.

The war against Zionism began in earnest after World War I. As Jews deepened their presence in the land, Arabs responded with increasing violence. Pogroms were imported from czarist Russia into Palestine. The worst occurred in 1929, in the holy city of Hebron, when sixty-nine unarmed Jews—members of the pious old *yishuv*—were butchered, many literally cut to pieces, by an Arab mob. At the same time, some four hundred Jews were saved by their Arab neighbors.

This event was a turning point in Zionist thinking. Until then many believed that coexistence was possible, even likely in the long term. After that, though, David Ben-Gurion and other Zionist leaders began preparing for protracted conflict.

Meanwhile, in the Arab world, the threats against its nearly one million Jews intensified. One of the most prominent Palestinian leaders, the Grand Mufti of Jerusalem, Haj Amin al-Husseini, spent World War II as Hitler's guest in Berlin, broadcasting appeals to the Muslim world to align with the Nazis and encouraging his hosts to extend the genocide from Europe to the Middle East. In a 1947 interview with an Egyptian newspaper, Azzam Pasha, secretary-general of the Arab League, warned the Jews not to create a state: "I hope the Jews do not force us into this war, because it would be a war of extermination and momentous massacre which will be spoken of like the Mongolian massacre and the Crusades." Azzam Pasha at least spoke with regret; other Arab leaders invoked the language of genocide with anticipation.

The final stage began on November 29, 1947, with the UN vote to establish "independent Arab and Jewish states," in the language of the General Assembly resolution. That decision was accepted by most of the Zionist movement and rejected by the entirety of the Palestinian national movement, which declared war against the Jewish presence. The day after the UN vote, Jews were attacked throughout the country. And when Israel was established six months later, on May 14, 1948, five Arab armies invaded, with the intent of destroying the Jewish state at birth.

Your side's narrative of those events was summed up by Palestinian leader Mahmoud Abbas in a *New York Times* op-ed in 2011. Shortly after the UN partition vote, writes Abbas, "Zionist forces expelled Palestinian Arabs to ensure a decisive Jewish majority in the future state of Israel, and Arab armies intervened. War and further expulsions ensued."

Israeli Jews read Abbas's words and seethe. What about the Zionist acceptance of partition, Mr. Abbas? And the Palestinian rejection of partition? What about the widespread and unprovoked Palestinian attacks against Jewish communities immediately after the

UN vote? And did Arab armies "intervene" to try to help the Palestinians or to fulfill their leaders' repeated vows to destroy the Jewish state?

An American Muslim friend once explained to me why Arab and Muslim nations unanimously rejected partition. The UN, he said, was in those years a white man's club, which had no right to divide up land in the Middle East, just as the British Balfour Declaration in 1917 had no right to grant the Jews any part of Palestine.

Yet the Jews hardly needed the international community's agreement to prove the justness of our claim. The Israeli Declaration of Independence cites Jewish historical roots and attachment to the land as proof of our legitimacy—"The land of Israel was the birthplace of the Jewish people," it begins—and only afterward notes the UN's endorsement of a Jewish state. The UN didn't "give" the Jews a state, any more than the British "gave" us our indigenous rights; our claim to the land comes from our very being. It came from those Jews who built the infrastructure of the emerging state—which existed in all but name by the time of the UN vote. It came from those Jews who fought an underground war and expelled the British occupiers, in one of the Middle East's most successful anticolonialist revolts.

Defenders of the Arab rejection of partition note that the UN plan awarded 55 percent of the land to the Jews, though they were still a minority. That objection, though, ignores the fact that more than half the landmass of the designated Jewish state was desert, while the designated Arab state contained the most fertile land. But would any partition plan have been acceptable to the Arab side? Had the Jewish state been given only a fraction of the land, the Arab world would almost certainly still have rejected partition, because any form of Jewish sovereignty in this land was regarded as a crime.

For me the compelling Palestinian argument against partition is the more straightforward one. As I've often heard Palestinians put it: If a stranger squatted in your home, would you accept dividing the house with him? Even if he gave you three rooms and kept "only" two, would you regard that compromise as fair?

Part of me empathizes with that position. I grew up in the right-wing Zionist youth movement, Betar— the maximalist movement of Jabotinsky and Menachem Begin—which also rejected the UN partition plan. I was thirteen years old when I joined Betar, and its uncompromising insistence that all the land belonged by right to us deeply stirred me. As a teenager I wore a necklace holding a small silver map of the land of Israel, as we understood it—including not only the West Bank but the territory that became the kingdom of Jordan, which the British had severed from historic Palestine and awarded to the Hashemites. Who were the British, we demanded, to decide the fate of our ancestral land? "Both banks of the Jordan are ours," we sang, "this one and the other, too."

I was so consumed by the justness of my people's claim that I couldn't hear your people's counterclaim. Older, in my twenties, I began asking subversive questions: How do Palestinians perceive this conflict? What is the basis of their argument? Curiosity led to empathy—the great enemies of self-righteousness. Finally came the realization that compromise—whether in one's personal life or in the life of a nation—offers a kind of fulfillment no less "authentic" than maximalist positions.

But in 1948, as our two peoples fought a war each perceived as one of national survival, neither could afford empathy. This was total war, with little distinction between civilians and combatants. The bitter fighting occurred on roads and in villages and on city streets, from house to house. There were massacres against both sides.

When I mention to Palestinians the massacres committed by your side, the usual response is: Yes, but your side started the war; we were only responding. Israeli Jews would say exactly the same. Wherever Arab armies were victorious, not a single Jew was left in place. Jews whose families had lived for centuries in East Jerusalem neighborhoods were expelled. Elsewhere Jews who were captured by Arab fighters were massacred, their communities uprooted. That was the choice: expulsion or slaughter.

In the war between us, each side had an advantage. Your side had the backing of five neighboring armies. Our side began the war with three tanks and four combat planes. And we were alone. But that, as it turned out, was a crucial advantage, because desperation forced us to mobilize our entire society for a war of survival. If your side had prevailed, few if any Jews would have been left here. As a result, the Jews fought with such determination that only a handful of our communities fell. There was nowhere left to run; we'd reached the final shore of Jewish history.

In the end, of course, it was your side that suffered the most devastating consequences. Some 700,000 Palestinians became refugees.

After the war, two competing narratives about the refugee tragedy emerged. For many years our side claimed that there had been no expulsion, only voluntary flight from battle, and that Arab leaders had encouraged Palestinians to abandon their homes, to clear the way for the imminently victorious Arab armies. Your side claimed that expulsion had been the norm, a systematic and premeditated Zionist plan.

Both versions were untrue. A new generation of Israeli historians proved that many of the refugees were in fact expelled by Israeli forces. While some Arab leaders did encourage Palestinians to flee, the line between flight and expulsion wasn't always clear. Many fled because they feared expulsion or massacre.

The refugee tragedy wasn't the result of a systematic Israeli policy, but often of decisions made by local commanders. In one case Prime Minister Ben-Gurion did explicitly order expulsion—from Lydda and Ramle, near Tel Aviv; and the expulsion from Lydda was accompanied by a massacre. Some Arab villages that kept out of the fighting were left alone. And in the mixed Jewish-Arab city of Haifa, the Jewish mayor stood in the street and pleaded with fleeing Arabs to remain. As the fighting intensified, tens of thousands of middle-class Palestinians fled, seeking safety, hoping to return after the Jews' defeat. Their departure only further demoralized Palestinian society. Many of your people were expelled, many fled—and some remained, which is why there are, today, over a million and a half Palestinian citizens of Israel, descendants of families who stayed. (About 150,000 remained after Israel's founding.)

Still, by the end of the war, it was your society that was shattered. Israel destroyed over four hundred emptied Palestinian villages, and Jewish refugees, many from Arab countries, were resettled on many of those sites. Palestinian refugees were dispersed in Syria and Lebanon and Jordan, in the Jordanian-held West Bank and the Egyptian-held Gaza Strip. As we Israelis celebrated our reclaimed sovereignty and achieved one success after another, your people exchanged homes and olive orchards for the scorched earth of refugee camps, where you raised children without hope, the unwanted outcasts of the Arab world. I mourn the lives wasted in the bitterness of exile, your despair against my joy.

But I cannot apologize for surviving. What almost any Israeli Jew will tell you is that if the Palestinian and Arab leadership had accepted compromise instead of declaring a war to the death, the Palestinian tragedy would not have happened.

There's another reason why Israeli Jews refuse to be cast as criminals in the story of 1948. At least half of Israel's population is rooted in the ancient Jewish communities of the Middle East. Within two decades following the creation of Israel, those thriving centers of Jewish life were almost entirely erased. Jews either fled violent anti-Semitism—a form of expulsion—or left of their own will, partly out of fear of anti-Jewish outbreaks and partly out of longing for Zion. Anti-Jewish pogroms throughout the 1940s—in Baghdad and Benghazi and Aleppo and other Arab cities—took hundreds of lives and created the atmosphere of terror that led to mass flight. Jews were stripped of their property, imprisoned, and hanged. The invisible refugees, Mizrahi Jews called themselves. Nearly one million Jews lived in the Muslim world in 1948; today, barely 40,000 remain.

One of my favorite Hebrew songs is called "The Village of Todra," a dirge for the lost culture of Moroccan Jews. It tells of a ritual, now vanished along with the Jewish communities of the Atlas Mountains, in which a Jewish boy is brought to the synagogue, where Hebrew letters on a wooden board are written in honey; the boy is told to lick, so that the words of Torah will be sweet in his mouth. Behind that charming recounting of a folkloristic custom is rage—against the destruction of a world.

Israelis sometimes compare Israel/Palestine to India/Pakistan. With the partition of India in 1947, millions of Hindus and Muslims fled in either direction across the border. There were frightful massacres on both sides—far more extensive than anything Jews and Arabs experienced.

The comparison with our conflict is inexact: Unlike India and Pakistan, where refugees on both sides found a haven in their own homelands, here only Jews fleeing Arab countries came to their homeland. The Jewish refugees were initially placed in immigrant shantytowns, and then resettled in housing projects and farming communities. There was, in those years, much discrimination against Mizrahim, Jews from Muslim countries, and the wounds of that period remain deep in Israeli society. But for all of Israel's many mistakes in absorbing the Mizrahim, they were regarded even by a patronizing Israeli establishment as *olim*, "ascenders" to the land of their ancestors.

Though Palestinian refugees fled to neighboring countries that share their religion and language, they were leaving their homeland for exile, the reverse of the Jews from Arab countries. Palestinian refugees were, for the most part, treated as strangers. Their plight requires a solution. And Israel, along with the Arab world, shares responsibility for healing this wound. Israel will need to pay compensation to the descendants of Palestinian refugees, just as Arab countries will need to pay compensation to the descendants of Jewish refugees.

The half million Jews who founded and defended Israel in 1948 may well have been the most remarkable Jewish community in history. They were builders, revolutionaries, mystics; writers and poets renewing a dead language, utopians dreaming of redeeming the world. They quarreled bitterly over how to achieve independence and over the nature of the future Jewish state. They lived with the acute awareness of their historical time, of carrying a broken people on their backs.

When I was a boy my friends and I would ask each other: If you could be born at any time in the past, which period of Jewish history would you want to live in? My answer was: in the time just before the creation of Israel, among the Zionists who were preparing the way for our national rebirth.

The challenges those young men and women confronted were as daunting as any ever faced by the founders of a nation. They had to not only liberate their society from foreign (British) rule but create that society from its foundations. They had to resurrect a language, modernize a culture without destroying its essence, and re-create a people from the most disparate communities.

Meanwhile, the Jewish people in the mid-twentieth century faced ruin. In Europe, Jews were being shipped to death camps. In the Middle East, they were under increasing threat of mob violence. In the Soviet Union, they were being forcibly assimilated by government decree.

That was the state of the Jewish people that the Zionists faced in the early 1940s. Through a combination of faith and realism, they salvaged their people and renewed its history.

But for all the love and admiration I feel toward the generation of Israel's founders, I live in a different time, which presents its own opportunities for transcendence. Unlike Ben-Gurion's generation, whose tasks of state building required a turning inward, a relentless self-absorption, the challenge facing my generation of Israelis is to turn outward—to you, neighbor, because my future is inseparable from yours.

There may well be no way to bridge our opposing narratives about the founding of Israel. Even as we seek a two-state solution, we will likely remain with a two-narrative problem. But that historical divide must not prevent a political compromise. I honor history—up to the point where it no longer inspires but imprisons. Accommodating both our narratives, learning to live with two contradictory stories, is the only way to deny the past a veto over the future.

It is late at night as I write you. On your hill only a few houses are lit. A forlorn car interrupts the quiet of the road between our hills. Reaching out to you, imagining an interlocutor across the way, makes me feel a little less alone in this silence.

I hear the predawn call of the muezzin or, rather, multiple calls from minarets on surrounding hills, not quite in sync, echoing each other. *Allahu akbar,* God is great. I am soothed by the quietly insistent voices, a gentle awakening, preparation for the imminent stirring of the day. "Prayer is preferred to sleep," they call out. Remember: We are here only temporarily; don't be a sleepwalker through your own life—don't waste your time, caught in the illusion of permanence. And then, abruptly, silence.

We live in such intimacy, we can almost hear each other breathing. What choice do we have but to share this land? And by that I mean share conceptually as well as tangibly. We must learn to accommodate each other's narratives. That is why I persist in writing to you, why I am trying to reach out across the small space and vast abyss that separates your hill from mine.

# Six Days and Fifty Years

Dear Neighbor,

Today is Jerusalem Day, commemorating the reunification of the city on June 7, 1967, during the Six-Day War. A hot wind rises from the desert. Later today the aging veterans of the battle for Jerusalem—left-wingers and right-wingers, secular and religious—will gather in quiet ceremonies around stone memorials in the streets of East Jerusalem, where the fighting occurred, and recall fallen friends and recite psalms. Elsewhere in East Jerusalem, young right-wing Jews will sing and dance through Palestinian neighborhoods, proclaiming the oneness of the city under Israeli control. Several coexistence groups appealed to the Supreme Court to reroute the march, but the court ruled for freedom of expression. I regret the ruling. Sometimes even sacred principles need to be tempered, to accommodate others' needs and sensibilities. That challenge, after all, helps define our conflict.

My encounter with Israel began in the weeks just before the Six-Day War. It was mid-May 1967, and Israel was being threatened with destruction. Arab leaders promised to drive the Jews into the sea. I watched on TV as crowds of demonstrators in Cairo and Damascus chanted, "Death to the Jews," and waved banners imprinted with skulls and crossbones. That was my first shock: The genocidal threat against the Jewish people hadn't ended with the Holocaust.

Egyptian president Gamal Abdel Nasser blockaded the Straits of Tiran, Israel's southern shipping route to the east, and expelled UN peacekeeping troops on the border with Israel. That was my second shock. Wasn't the purpose of peacekeeping forces to be in place for precisely a moment like this? And yet the UN complied with Nasser's demand to remove the peacekeepers, without so much as a debate in the Security Council.

The Syrian and Jordanian armies joined together with the Egyptians, encircling Israel. Hundreds of thousands of Israeli reservists were called up, crippling the economy of a country with barely three million citizens at the time. High school students were sent to dig mass graves in parks, preparing for thousands of civilian casualties. Overwhelmed by the threat, Yitzhak Rabin, the chief of staff of the Israel Defense Forces (IDF), suffered a temporary nervous breakdown. Jews around the world feared Israel's imminent destruction.

I discovered something essential about myself in those days: I couldn't live in a world without Israel. That realization may sound strange to you, neighbor. I was, after all, a thirteen-year-old boy in Brooklyn. Why this primal attachment, so intense that I was ready at that moment to give my life for a country I had never visited?

It was, I think, the intuitive sense that the Jewish people wouldn't survive the destruction of Israel. Not that the Jews would suddenly vanish: Jewish communities around the world would continue to exist. But the life force, the self-confidence, the ability to dream in history, the belief in a Jewish story—all would dissipate. The longing that sustained us through adversity would be exposed as ludicrous: We had waited two thousand years for an event that turned out to be one more Jewish nightmare. We'd gathered in Zion from around the world not for redemption but for the ultimate destruction.

True, the Jews had survived previous loss of our national sovereignty. But when the Judean state was destroyed in 70 CE, we were still a people of active faith. We fashioned from the broken pieces a new pattern of Jewish life because we knew how to interpret our fate through a religious lens. Paradoxically, the belief that the Jews had been punished by God gave our ancestors the courage to persist. The same God Who punished would also one day redeem. The prison term would be served and exile would end. Today, though, we live in the aftermath of the shattering of Jewish faith, brought on in part by Western secularism and the Holocaust. Whatever faith has managed to survive our experiences in the modern world would be tested to the breaking point by the destruction of Israel. Few Jews, I suspect, would accept another narrative of Divine punishment. Even for many religious Jews, this would be one punishment too many.

On the morning of June 5, 1967, I awoke to see my father hovering over the kitchen radio. War had begun. We didn't know it then, but the Israeli air force had preemptively struck, destroying almost the entire Egyptian air force while its planes were parked on the ground.

Israel sent a message to King Hussein of Jordan: Stay out of the fighting, and so will we. But Jordanian army units based in East Jerusalem began shelling

Jewish neighborhoods in West Jerusalem. A brigade of Israeli paratroopers was dispatched to the city and, with only hours to organize, crossed the municipal no-man's-land of minefields and barbed wire and attacked Jordanian positions. The goal was to stop the firing on West Jerusalem and to protect the Israeli enclave of Mount Scopus in East Jerusalem. There were no contingency plans for the IDF to take the Old City. Even as Israeli paratroopers surrounded the Old City's walls, the Israeli government hesitated to give the order to invade—though the area contains the holiest Jewish sites, to which we'd been denied access ever since the Jordanians seized them in 1948.

The decision, reached after long debate in the Israeli cabinet, came on the morning of June 7—but not before the government sent one last appeal to King Hussein, offering to call off the paratroopers in exchange for peace talks. Hussein ignored the overture. Paratroopers then broke through the Lions' Gate of the Old City, turned left into the area we call the Temple Mount and you call Haram el Sharif, the Noble Sanctuary, and reached the Western Wall.

I don't know if there was a Jew alive, no matter how distanced from faith, who was indifferent to the sight of exhausted Jewish paratroopers leaning their heads into the crevices of the Wall that had been the repository of the prayers of exile. The iconic image of that moment is a photograph of several paratroopers, arms around each other's shoulders, standing at the Wall and gazing upward. Though they'd just won the greatest military victory in Jewish history, their young faces revealed not triumph but awe, like pilgrims at the end of a journey. At that moment they weren't representing the might of a sovereign state but the hopes of an ancient people.

A few weeks after the war, my father and I flew to Israel for the first time. We simply couldn't keep away. And there I fell in love. With the landscape, of course, the diversity of desert and mountain and coast, planet Earth seemingly condensed into a single strip. But most of all I was enchanted by the diversity of the Jews. Living in a neighborhood in Brooklyn where the range of Jewish ethnicity was basically covered by the Austro-Hungarian Empire, I was thrilled to encounter Jews from Morocco and Iraq and India and dozens of other countries, stretching my sense of Jewish possibility. Exile had shattered us into multiple fragments, and now the impossible was happening: however awkwardly, even traumatically, the fragments were reassembling. I fell in love with the Israelis— their courage, their hard decency. They were ready to make the best of whatever circumstances history dealt them. Like my teenage cousin, also named Yossi, who lived on the shore of the Sea of Galilee, and who had grown up swimming under the guns of Syrian soldiers on the Golan Heights, and who accepted as a fact of life that he would soon become a soldier.

I wasn't blind to the flaws in the Israeli character: the rudeness, the provincialism, the petty materialism of a poor nation. But those were mere details; my love was unconditional. That summer I resolved that, no matter what happened in my life or in the life of Israel, I would return one day as an immigrant.

But in the midst of that summer's celebration of victory, of life itself—there you were, the mourner at the wedding. Strips of white cloth hung in surrender from Palestinian homes. Old men leading donkeys moved slowly, as if carrying great loads. Children with heads shaved against lice sold hastily carved wooden camels, soda bottles with colored swirling sand, picture postcards of Israel's defense minister, Moshe Dayan—mementos of your defeat. Perhaps you, neighbor, were one of those children. I tried to forget their faces, suppress pity, remind myself that we'd barely escaped annihilation. Just imagine, Israelis said to each other, what they would have done to us if *they* had won. In a Palestinian refugee camp in El Arish, I saw paintings by children envisioning that victory: Arab soldiers shooting ultra-Orthodox Jews, a pile of skulls with Jewish stars. Still, not even those images can erase the sullen and confused young faces I'd seen on the streets of East Jerusalem. When I close my eyes, I can see them even now.

The map of Israel changed again. Israel's borders expanded in three stages: first, through the land purchases in the pre-state era, then in the 1948 War—and finally, in the Six-Day War. Most of the international community has accepted the first two stages as legitimate—and negotiations between Israeli and Palestinian leaders have been based on the borders of Israel as they emerged in 1949. As far as the international community is concerned, it is the third stage of territorial acquisition that is being contested.

The first West Bank settlement—Kfar Etzion, just south of Jerusalem on the road to Hebron—was founded in September 1967, barely three months after the war. There was no parliamentary debate, no cabinet decision, no grand expansionist plan: simply a dozen young people moving to a hilltop, with the ambiguous consent of then prime minister Levi Eshkol. The reason for the lack of controversy was that the original Kfar Etzion had been destroyed in the 1948 War and those young people, who'd been born there and were evacuated as children just before it fell, were literally returning home. Kfar Etzion was one of the open wounds of the Israeli psyche: Its defenders had surrendered to Palestinian militiamen and were massacred the day before Israel's declaration of independence. And so the first West Bank settlement restored a Jewish community that had existed in modern times. This wasn't, at least initially, about reclaiming a biblical heritage but, for the Israeli public, about undoing a wrong within living memory.

Six months later a group of settlers moved into Hebron—Judaism's second-holiest city, after Jerusalem. This time there was a vehement debate among Israelis—about the wisdom of inserting Jews into a major Palestinian population center. Hebron, burial place of Abraham and Sarah, is of course the basis for the Jewish biblical claim to the land. And yet Hebron, too, was a kind of modern restoration: After the 1929 massacre, its ancient Jewish community disappeared.

The first two settlements, then, were reconstructions of Jewish communities destroyed in the twentieth century. That helps explain why many Israelis failed to perceive those initial settlements as the beginning of a mass movement. The settlers, of course, well understood the long-term implications of their acts. Perhaps you did, too.

Immediately after the Six-Day War, the Arab League, representing the entire Arab world, reaffirmed its emphatic rejection of Israel's existence, and that, too, helped legitimize settlements for many Israelis. One of the leaders of the settlement movement, the late professor of Jewish philosophy Yosef Ben-Shlomo, began his political involvement by signing a public letter opposing the reestablishment of the Jewish community of Hebron. But, he later explained, when he realized that the Arab world wasn't prepared to accept Israel's legitimacy in any borders, he came to believe that a land-for-peace agreement was naive.

Palestinian terrorism reinforced the message to Israelis that there was no chance for compromise. Yasser Arafat's men blew up a school bus, seized high school students as hostages, massacred pilgrims at Israel's international airport, slaughtered families in their homes, smashed the head of a child against a rock, murdered bound members of the Israeli Olympic team. Israelis experienced those attacks as small pre-enactments of the genocidal aim of the Palestinian national movement, proof that compromise was impossible.

Still, through the early 1970s, the Labor Party, then Israel's undisputed party of governance, kept settlement building in the West Bank to a minimum. Labor was committed to reaching an agreement to return territory to Jordan, which claimed to speak for the Palestinian cause. When settlement groups squatted in the territories, the Labor-led government dispatched the army to break up their encampments.

Labor's ability to control the settlement movement began to unravel on a precise date—November 10, 1975. That's when the UN, voting 72 to 35 with 32 abstentions, declared Zionism a form of racism—the only national movement ever singled out for such opprobrium. The bloc of Muslim states, together with the Communist world, meant that any anti-Israel resolution was assured of passage.

In response, thousands of young Israelis gathered around an abandoned Ottoman railway station in Samaria, in the northern West Bank, pitched tents in the winter mud, and posted a sign: ZIONISM AVENUE. A freshman Knesset member named Ehud Olmert told a journalist: This is the real Zionist answer to the UN. (In 2008, as prime minister of Israel, Olmert would offer your leaders a state on almost all of the West Bank and Gaza.) The Labor government, which had always reacted to similar protests by ordering the army to remove squatters, now hesitated. Public opinion shifted toward the settlers—thanks to the UN vote. Rather than evict the squatters, the government offered a compromise, and a group of settlers moved into an army base.

Of course, there were other more important factors, besides the UN resolution, that eventually led to the empowerment of the settlement movement—especially the 1977 electoral victory of the rightwing Likud. But the Israeli public's response to the UN resolution tells us something essential about the Israeli character: When we feel unfairly stigmatized, we toughen our position. The greatest beneficiary of attempts to isolate and delegitimize Israel is the hard Right.

But the opposite is no less true: When Israel's legitimacy is respected, Israelis tend to take risks for peace. That's what happened in 1977, when President Anwar Sadat of Egypt came to Jerusalem and declared his acceptance of Israel. In response, the Israeli public supported a total withdrawal from the Sinai desert, which Israel had occupied in the Six-Day War, including uprooting all its settlements. Then, in the early 1990s, with the fall of the Soviet Union and the Communist bloc, the UN voted to repeal the Zionism-racism resolution, and dozens of countries established diplomatic relations with Israel. The change in Israel's status was one reason why the Israeli government felt confident to initiate the Oslo peace process, and why a majority of Israelis at least initially supported it.

For many Israelis in the aftermath of the Six-Day War, the arguments for settling the territories seemed overwhelming. After all, we had returned to the historic heart of our homeland through a war of self-defense against attempted destruction. A withdrawal from the West Bank would reduce the Jewish state to vulnerable borders that had repeatedly tempted Arab states to attack us. The Arab rejection of Israel's legitimacy increased the likelihood that sooner or later our neighbors would try again, regardless of whatever piece of paper their leaders signed. And what people, in our place, would have resisted reclaiming land it regarded as its own for thousands of years?

Yet the counterargument was no less compelling. There were voices warning against settling "the territories," as many ambivalent Israelis called them, even in the heady summer of 1967. The young Amos Oz, later to become one of Israel's leading novelists, wrote a powerful essay that summer warning that there is no such thing as a benign occupation or "liberated territories." Only people, wrote Oz, can be liberated, not land.

The success of the settlement movement is a result of the convergence of Israel's security fears with the call of history. I, too, felt that pull after moving to Israel in the early 1980s, when many of the settlements were founded. Rationally, I understood that Amos Oz was right, that this would likely turn out to be a disaster not only for your side but also for mine. And yet, as a reporter covering the settlements, I involuntarily thrilled to the sight of new white houses rising against the white hills, the courage of young Israelis defying the world to stake our claim—the very spirit, I felt, that had helped us survive as a people. A friend invited me to the ceremony of the founding of his settlement, on the site of biblical Tekoa, near Bethlehem, on the edge of a desert valley. A banner proclaimed the words of the prophet Amos, "the man of Tekoa," as the Bible calls him: "I will restore my people, Israel; they shall rebuild the ruined cities and inhabit them. And I will plant them on their land, nevermore to be uprooted from the land I have given them, says the Lord your God." At that moment, the fulfillment of those words recorded some 2,500 years ago and being played out before me tempered my misgivings.

Nowhere in this land did I feel more like a returning son than when I went on pilgrimage to Hebron. I love Tel Aviv, its informal vitality, its ability to continually redefine itself, but by the standards of Jewish history and of the Middle East, Tel Aviv is a baby city, barely a century old. In Hebron, though, I felt embraced by all who came before me, all who prayed in the multiple accents of exile to the God of Abraham and Sarah.

I write about "returning" to Hebron, but in fact we never voluntarily left. The Jewish imprint on Hebron wasn't only biblical—it continued through the centuries of exile. The evidence left behind is in the medieval Jewish cemetery, in the sixteenth-century Avraham Avinu (Our Father Abraham) Synagogue, destroyed after the 1929 pogrom and turned into an animal pen, and in the indentations where mezuzahs were ripped from the doorposts.

How could Jews not live in Hebron? Emotionally I agreed with the settlers: If we didn't belong here, we didn't belong anywhere.

Ironically, it was in Hebron that my romance with the settlement movement ended. On an autumn night in 1984, I went to report on a Jewish celebration that was happening in the streets of Hebron. It was the night after Simchat Torah, the festival when Jews dance with Torah scrolls to mark the completion of the annual cycle of biblical readings in the synagogue. Some Jews prolong the dancing for one more night, which is what the settlers were doing then. It is a beautiful custom, merging reverence with joy. But it was not beautiful that night in Hebron. To accommodate the celebration, the army had shut the streets and placed

Palestinian residents under curfew. I saw Jews raising Torah scrolls, which contain the injunction to remember that we were strangers in Egypt and so we must treat the stranger fairly, dancing in the streets emptied of their Palestinian neighbors. The insistence on empathy with the stranger appears with greater frequency in the Torah than any other verse—including commandments to observe the Sabbath and keep kosher.

That curfew became for me a metaphor for the fatal flaw of the settlement movement: the sin of not seeing, of becoming so enraptured with one's own story, the justice and poetry of one's national epic, that you can't acknowledge the consequences to another people of fulfilling the whole of your own people's dreams.

I believe deeply in our historical and religious claim to Hebron—to all of the land of Israel between the Jordan River and the Mediterranean Sea. For me, that land isn't "occupied territory" but Judea and Samaria, which is how Jews have called it since biblical times. Jews in Judea are not aliens. But like many Israelis, I am ready to partition the land—if convinced the trade-off will be peace, and not greater terror. For those of us who support a two-state solution, ensuring the security of Israel—and not implementing historical claims—is the most important measure for deciding the fate of the territories. For me there is only one legitimate reason for deferring partition of the land we share: if it would place Israel in mortal danger.

In 1989, at the height of the first intifada, I was drafted into the IDF. My unit was eventually sent into the Gaza refugee camps, and that's where I learned the meaning of occupation. By day we would enter the camps—shantytowns of corrugated roofs held down with blocks, sewage running in ditches—to demonstrate a presence, as the army put it. By night we would search homes for terror suspects—or for those who hadn't paid, say, their water bills. We weren't soldiers as much as policemen, enforcing an occupation that seemed to me increasingly untenable.

Late one night we knocked on a door beside a wall covered with anti-Israel graffiti. A groggy middle-aged man answered. Paint over the graffiti, we ordered. We shined the light of our jeep on the wall and silently watched as he and his sons painted over the offensive words.

A grenade was thrown at soldiers near an outdoor market. Though it didn't explode, the order was given: Shut down the stalls. We politely asked vendors to close. Most of us were older recruits, and we were abashed before these men, fathers like us who only wanted to feed their families. Sensing our reluctance, the vendors ignored us. An officer appeared. Wordlessly he approached a stand selling lemons and emptied the contents on the ground. The market cleared.

A chubby teenage Palestinian boy, accused of stone throwing, was brought, blindfolded, into our tent camp. A group of soldiers from the Border Police unit gathered around. One said to him in Arabic, Repeat after me: One order of hummus, one order of fava beans, I love the Border Police. The young man dutifully repeated the rhymed Arabic ditty. There was laughter.

That last story haunts me most of all. It is, seemingly, insignificant. The prisoner wasn't physically abused; his captors, young soldiers under enormous strain, shared a joke. But that incident embodies for me the corruption of occupation. When my son was about to be drafted into the army I told him: There are times when as a soldier you may have to kill. But you are never permitted, under any circumstances, to humiliate another human being. That is a core Jewish principle.

Along with many Israelis of my generation, I emerged from the first intifada convinced that Israel must end the occupation—not just for your sake but for ours. Free ourselves from the occupation, which mocked all we held precious about ourselves as a peo-

ple. Justice, mercy, empathy: These were the foundations of Jewish life for millennia. "Justice, justice, shall
you pursue," the Torah commands us, emphasizing the
word "justice." "Merciful children of merciful parents," we traditionally called our fellow Jews.

Occupation penetrates the soul. When I first got to
Gaza, the army slang offended me. Soldiers referred to
one camp as "Amsterdam" because of the open sewage canals; they called the sand lot that passed for the
central square of another camp "Dizengoff," a central
square in Tel Aviv. After a few weeks, I, too, adopted
the slang mocking Gaza's misery.

Perhaps, neighbor, you are asking yourself: Why is
this Israeli telling *me* about the meaning of occupation?
I am sharing with you my experience as occupier because I believe that if our two societies are someday to
coexist as equal neighbors, we need to begin talking
about this prolonged ordeal that has bound us together
in pathological entwinement.

I learned something else in Gaza: The dream of
Palestine wasn't only to be free of Israeli occupation
but to be free of Israel's existence entirely. Graffiti
promised death to the Jews. The most persistent image
on Gaza's walls was of knives and swords plunging into
a map of Israel, dripping blood.

One of my close friends in the unit was Shimon

from Ethiopia. I've already told you about Shimon, who limped because a Sudanese soldier had crushed his bare foot. Shimon felt none of my ambivalence in Gaza: He was there to defend his family and his country from Gaza's dream of Israel's disappearance. They want to destroy us, he said to me, they want to return us to the refugee camp in Sudan. Shimon was not going to allow Gaza to undo the fulfillment of his people's dream.

I veered between moral and existential fears. Both seemed to me reasonable—essential—Jewish responses to Gaza, to our Palestinian dilemma. Jewish history, I believed, spoke to my generation with two nonnegotiable commandments. The first was to remember that we'd been strangers in the land of Egypt and the message was: Be compassionate. The second commandment was to remember that we live in a world in which genocide is possible, and that message was: Be alert. When your enemy says he intends to destroy you, believe him.

What makes my dilemma so excruciating is that those two nonnegotiable commandments of Jewish history converge on our conflict: The stranger whom we are occupying is the enemy who intends to dispossess us. And so how do I relate to you, neighbor: as victim or as would-be victimizer?

In 1992 Yitzhak Rabin, head of the Labor Party, was elected prime minister. Rabin had run on the campaign slogan "Take Tel Aviv out of Gaza and Gaza out of Tel Aviv." In other words, an Israeli withdrawal from Gaza. Rabin deeply moved me. The commander of the IDF in the Six-Day War was returning as an elder statesman to extricate us from the dilemmas he had bequeathed to us as a young man.

The night Rabin was elected, I wept with relief. Finally: Here was our chance to end the occupation. A year later, when Rabin shook Arafat's hand at the White House and began the Oslo peace process, I agonized: Was this a breakthrough to peace or had we just committed one of the greatest mistakes in our history? Arafat had devoted his life to the destruction of Israel, to undermining our legitimacy. No one in this generation had more Jewish blood on his hands. But if Rabin was ready to gamble on Arafat the peacemaker, then so was I.

Yet Arafat and the leaders of what became the Palestinian Authority gradually convinced Israelis that their diplomacy was in fact war by other means. Arafat created his own diplomatic language: To CNN he spoke about the peace of the brave, while exhorting his people to holy war. Meanwhile, Hamas intensified terror attacks against Israeli civilians. Israeli intelligence warned Rabin that Arafat was secretly encouraging Hamas and had created a division of labor: Hamas would continue the violence while Arafat won territory through negotiations.

For many Israelis, the turning point was Arafat's 1994 speech in a Johannesburg mosque. Though the speech was off-limits to the media, a journalist smuggled in a tape recorder. Arafat reassured his critics in the Arab world that he really had no intention of making peace, that the only reason he entered into peace talks was that the Palestinians were too weak for now to seriously threaten Israel and that the Oslo process was nothing more than a cease-fire, to be broken at the appropriate time. The transcript of that talk made headlines in Israel. Arafat's defenders tried to reassure Israelis: He's just playing to the crowd. But the cumulative impact of Arafat's rhetoric reinforced the deepest Israeli fears of being deceived, of lowering our guard.

Like most Israelis, I came to believe we'd been played for fools. A two-state solution had never been Arafat's intention—except as prelude to a one-state solution, the end of the Jewish people's dream of sovereignty. For Israel there would be no peace, only territorial withdrawals accompanied by terrorism. The Israeli Right was vindicated: More Israeli concessions led to more terror.

In supporting the Oslo process, I had violated one of the commanding voices of Jewish history, the warning against naïveté. I had confused war for peace, one big Palestine for two smaller states.

Rather than view our conflict as a tragedy being played out between two legitimate national movements—as many Israelis have come to see it—the uncontested official narrative on the Palestinian side defines the conflict as colonialists versus natives. And the fate of the colonialist, as modern history has proven and justice demands, is to ultimately be expelled from the lands he has stolen. Tel Aviv no less than Gaza.

The Israeli novelist A. B. Yehoshua has called our conflict a struggle between "right and right." Where is the Palestinian A. B. Yehoshua to echo that tragic insight? In the Israeli media, thousands of op-eds have appeared over the years demanding that Israelis face the reality of a competing narrative. I understand that it's far easier for the victor to show nuance than the vanquished. Still, in all the years I've been following Palestinian media, I don't recall a single op-ed or editorial in any publication, regardless of its political affiliation, advocating a reassessment of the Jewish narrative. Not one article among the daily media assault denying and ridiculing and denouncing my being.

And so most Israelis, even many on the left, have

concluded that, no matter what concessions Israel offers, the conflict will persist. The goal of the Palestinian national movement, Israelis are convinced, isn't just to undo the consequences of 1967—occupation and settlements—but the consequences of 1948—the existence of Israel. For those of us who believe in a two-state solution, that is a devastating realization.

Our conflict is defined by asymmetries. Israel is the most powerful nation in the Middle East, the Palestinians the least powerful. Yet we are alone in the region, while you are part of a vast Arab and Muslim hinterland. Those are the obvious asymmetries. Less obvious are the political differences on each side. Among Israelis, supporters of a two-state solution regard partition as the end of the conflict. But from years of conversation with Palestinians I learned that even supporters of two states often see that as a temporary solution resulting from Palestinian powerlessness, to be replaced with one state—with the Jews as a minority, if existing at all—once Palestinian refugees return and Israel begins to unravel. And where Israeli moderates tend to see Palestinian sovereignty as a necessary act of justice, many Palestinian moderates see Israeli sovereignty as an unavoidable injustice.

I can think of no national movement that has rejected more offers of statehood—going back to the

1930s—than the Palestinian national movement. And given its perception of Zionism and Israel, that's understandable. If Palestinians believe that Israel is the embodiment of evil and so must be destroyed—and there is no other reasonable conclusion to draw from the messages conveyed by Palestinian media and mosques and educational system—then genuine compromise becomes impossible.

If you were in my place, neighbor, what would you do? Would you take the chance and withdraw to narrow borders and trust a rival national movement that denied your right to exist? Would you risk your ability to defend yourself, perhaps your existence, to empower him? And would you do so while the region around you was burning?

Having concluded that every concession I offer will be turned against me, I remain in limbo, affirming a two-state solution while clinging to the status quo. And yet I cannot accept our current state of seemingly endless conflict as the definitive verdict on our relationship.

We are trapped, you and I, in a seemingly hopeless cycle. Not a "cycle of violence"—a lazy formulation that tells us nothing about why our conflict exists, let alone how to end it. Instead, we're trapped in what may be called a "cycle of denial." Your side denies my people's legitimacy, my right to self-determination, and my side prevents your people from achieving national sovereignty. The cycle of denial defines our shared existence, an impossible intimacy of violence, suppression, rage, despair.

That is the cycle we can only break together.

# The Partition of Justice

Dear Neighbor,

So how do we end the cycle of denial?

Borders and settlements and Jerusalem are all crucial problems that require solutions. But those tangible issues are only consequences of the intangible fears and longings that animate our conflict—survival and the right to exist, historical memory and the legitimacy of our national stories. No political formula or compromise, no arbitrary line on a map, can address each people's deepest anxieties. We need to acknowledge why a two-state solution is so traumatic for so many of us, Israelis and Palestinians alike.

The truth is, neighbor, I dread partition. As much as I tell myself that I want and need a two-state solution, emotionally I cringe at the prospect of cutting this tiny, beloved land into two sovereign states. The entire land between the Jordan River and the Mediterranean Sea—including the state of Israel, the West Bank, and Gaza—is less than 11,000 square miles.

I dread inflicting a self-imposed wound on the Jewish people. How do we abandon Hebron without doing violence to our most basic sense of Jewish history? In the past we were exiled by our enemies, and that somehow allowed us to accept our fate. This time, though, we will exile ourselves. How will we endure the bitterness? Of course, I understand that we would be giving up only a part of the historic land and in the process salvaging a Jewish and democratic state—and, hopefully, receiving some measure of peace in return. But emotionally I experience partition just as the settlers do: as self-mutilation.

I am deeply moved by the success of the settlement movement: the reemergence of native Judeans and Samarians. Children and now grandchildren have been born and raised in the rebuilt Jewish communities of Shilo and Ofra and Bet El and Kiryat Arba—the landmarks of our people's childhood. Those Israelis see their lives as undoing the wrongs of Jewish history, a belated answer to the Roman conquerors and to all who tried to erase us. They cherish their daily life as an affirmation of rootedness.

Over the last century, thousands of Jewish communities in Europe and in the Muslim world were destroyed. Are we ourselves to now destroy Jewish communities in the land of Israel—thriving towns and villages built around an organic Jewish life? I speak so casually about supporting a two-state solution. But how do I drag tens of thousands of my fellow Israelis from their homes and workplaces and schools? My generation was privileged to return to the lands that Jews, through the centuries of exile, dreamed of re-inhabiting. To be the generation that restored Jewish life to the hills of Judea and Samaria, only to uproot ourselves—voluntarily—will be a historic trauma.

I understand the Palestinian visceral rejection of the very word "Israel," because I feel the same way about "Palestine." Unlike many of my fellow Israelis, I am unfazed by the maps that omit the Jewish state that hang in your classrooms and offices, because on my emotional map there is no Palestine. How can a foreign name be imposed on my beloved land? Instinctively, I experience the very name "Palestine" as an act of linguistic aggression. It is like waking up one morning and learning that the name you carried since birth isn't yours after all and you've been forced into a new, alien identity.

The well-intentioned Western diplomats trying to

make peace between us don't understand: For both our peoples, partition isn't an ideal but a violation, an amputation. Israel without Hebron? Palestine without Jaffa? Inconceivable.

And yet—I see no sane alternative to partition. No matter how much each side tries to erase the other's map, Israel and Palestine persist. You and I inhabit a land that is, conceptually at least, two lands. Between the river and the sea lie the land of Israel and the land of Palestine. Tragically, those two entities happen to exist in the same space. If you tell me, neighbor, that Haifa belongs to you, my response is: I understand, from your perspective Haifa does belong to you. But the problem is that, from my perspective, Hebron belongs to me.

Given the failure of the peace process and the emotional resistance on both sides to partition, it is tempting to embrace a one-state solution, in which Palestinians and Israelis will somehow jointly govern. But those promoting that seeming solution are deceiving themselves. The only solution worse than dividing this land into two states is creating one state that would devour itself. No two peoples who have fought a hundred-year existential war can share the intimate workings of government. The current conflict between us would pale beside the rage that would erupt when competing for the same means of power. The most likely model is the disintegration of Yugoslavia into its warring ethnic and religious factions—perhaps even worse. A one-state solution would condemn us to a nightmare entwinement—and deprive us both of that which justice requires: self-determination, to be free peoples in our own sovereign homelands.

I need a Jewish state. Not a state only for Jews— even after partition a substantial minority of Palestinian citizens of Israel will remain in its borders—but a state where the public space is defined by Jewish culture and values and needs, where Jews from East and West can reunite and together create a new era of Jewish civilization. One corner of the planet where the holiday cycle begins on the Jewish new year and the radio sings in modern Hebrew and the history taught in schools is framed by the Jewish experience.

Israelis used to believe that we'd created a safe refuge for the Jewish people. These days, though, with tens of thousands of missiles aimed at our population centers, we're less certain. But Israel is a safe refuge for Judaism, for our four-thousand-year civilization. This is the only country where Jews are not concerned about disappearing into a non-Jewish majority culture.

A Muslim American friend of mine visiting Israel went to the Western Wall on a Jewish holiday and found himself in a crowd of thousands of Jews. Afterward he said to me, "Now I get why Jews need a state: to be able to protect your religious life and have your own pilgrimages, like we do in Mecca." "The Jewish hajj," he called it, a uniquely Muslim insight into Jewish sovereignty.

If Jaffa belongs to you and Hebron belongs to me, then we have two options. We can continue fighting for another hundred years, in the hope that one side or the other will prevail. Or we can accept the solution that has been on the table almost since the conflict began, and divide the land between us. In accepting partition, we are not betraying our histories, neighbor; we are conceding that history has given us no real choice.

David Ben-Gurion, who believed no less than the Zionist maximalists in the rightness of the Jewish claim to all of the historical land of Israel, nevertheless supported the UN partition plan in 1947. He noted that the peculiar circumstances of the Jewish return home after two thousand years required humility on the part of Zionism, a readiness to compromise even on what belonged to us.

How, then, to move from our mutually exclusive geographies and begin accommodating each other's maps? Perhaps by acknowledging that we both love this land in its wholeness, and that we both must do violence to that love. A peace agreement should frankly accept the legitimacy of each side's maximalist claims, even as it proceeds to contract them. Partition is an act of injustice to both Palestinians and Israelis. It is the recognition of the borders to our dreams. Not only the land but justice itself is being partitioned between two rightful claimants.

Neither side can relinquish its emotional claim to territorial wholeness. Yet not every claim must be implemented in full. The state of Israel cannot be identical with the land of Israel, the state of Palestine with the land of Palestine. Each people will exercise national sovereignty in only a part of its land. We need to separate the abstract justness of the entire claim from the practical injustice of its fulfillment. Neither side can implement the totality of its claim without erasing the claim of the other. The moral argument of partition, then, is simply this: For the sake of allowing the other side to achieve some measure of justice, each side needs to impose on itself some measure of injustice.

I envision a peace agreement in which each side stakes its claim to all of Israel/Palestine. But peace between us and partial justice for each, the agreement will conclude, require heartbreaking concessions. The enemy of justice for both sides is absolute justice for either side.

"Justice, justice, shall you pursue," commands the Torah. The rabbis ask: Why the repetition of the word "justice"? My answer has been shaped by our conflict: Sometimes, the pursuit of justice means fulfilling two claims to justice, even when they clash.

That requires a trade-off: I forfeit Greater Israel and you forfeit Greater Palestine. Partition will leave us diminished: lesser Israel, lesser Palestine. In the impairment of absolute justice will emerge a more wounded justice. But that justice will accommodate us both. As a great Hasidic teacher, Menachem Mendel of Kotzk, put it, "Nothing is more whole than a broken heart." For us, neighbor, nothing is more just than the brokenness of partition.

No doubt it would be easier for you to deal with the secular left-wing Israeli who repudiates an emotional claim to Judea and Samaria and refers to those lands as "occupied territories." But, for better or worse, I'm the Israeli you need to make peace with—precisely because I am in love with all parts of the land and loath to abandon any of it.

One reason to consider me your partner is practical: My sensibility is shared by a substantial part of the

Israeli public. But there's a deeper reason: My view mirrors your own notion of ownership. Almost every Palestinian I've met believes as a matter of course that all of the land belongs by right to your side. Peace can only be made when each side understands that the other has sacrificed some essential part of itself. Israelis like me can be your partner in the mutual pain of partition.

Much of the Israeli Left has committed the fatal mistake of emotionally withdrawing from Judea and Samaria and in effect renouncing our historic claim. Ironically, yet not illogically, the only Israeli leaders who ever initiated substantive withdrawals from the territories won in the Six-Day War were right-wingers. Menachem Begin withdrew from the Sinai desert in 1982 and became the first leader to uproot settlements; and in 2005, Ariel Sharon destroyed the settlements in Gaza he himself built. The pattern in Israeli politics has been that the Right implements the vision of the Left. The Left can't lead a withdrawal because, on matters of security, the public trusts only the Right. Israelis also want their leaders to feel genuine angst when ceding territory. Only those who would mourn the loss of the Israeli heartland and the destruction of its Jewish communities will be entrusted with that heartbreaking process.

The pursuit of partition has two nemeses. One is on my side: the settlement movement. The other is on your side: the demand for return of Palestinian refugees to the state of Israel. Both share the same goal: to deny the rival claimant national sovereignty in any part of this land. The settlement movement seeks to fill the West Bank with so many Israelis that withdrawal becomes impossible. And by linking a peace agreement to the return of descendants of the refugees of 1948, Palestinian leaders seek to fill Israel with so many Palestinians that Jews will eventually lose their majority and the Jewish state will cease to be.

I don't share the pessimists' conclusion that the settlement movement has won and that it's too late for Israel to extricate itself from the territories. Israel, after all, uprooted all its settlements in Gaza. And though there are many more settlers in the West Bank, a majority live close to the old 1967 border, and "settlement blocs" could be annexed by Israel, in exchange for equivalent Israeli territory to be ceded to Palestine—in areas partly bordering Gaza, partly bordering the West Bank.

One aspect of a possible solution would be to allow Jews to remain as citizens of a Palestinian state. Just as Arabs live within Israel as citizens, so, too, will Jews live within Palestine as citizens. Those who are

so attached to Judea and Samaria that they would pre-
fer minority status to uprooting should be allowed to
remain.

Withdrawal will require a strong leader committed
to an agreement and a determined Israeli majority—
and, to persuade skeptical Israelis, some sign of genuine Palestinian acceptance of a Jewish state. None of
those conditions exist today. But in the Middle East,
as we've learned, anything is possible. And if a final-
status agreement can't be achieved at this time, we
should consider an interim agreement.

A key obstacle to a final-status agreement remains
the "right of return"—the right of the descendants of
Palestinian refugees from 1948 to return to Palestine.
After reading what I wrote about the Jewish longing to
return home, you may well ask: Can't Jews, of all people, understand the longing of Palestinians to return?
Jews insisted on their right to return after two thousand years; how can they deny the right of Palestinians
to return after barely seventy years?

I accept your right of return. But the question is,
To where? Israelis who support a two-state solution
envision return to that part of the homeland that will
become a sovereign Palestinian state. But Palestinian
leaders have demanded that the right of return include
what is now the state of Israel.

We are both peoples with extensive diasporas. In 1950 the new state of Israel passed the "Law of Return," guaranteeing automatic citizenship to any Jew coming home from any part of the world, under any circumstances. That's how I became an Israeli: I showed up one day at Ben-Gurion Airport and declared myself a returning son. The Law of Return is the foundation on which the Jewish state stands, defining its moral responsibility to the Jewish people. The state of Palestine will surely enact a similar law for your people. A law of return is an immigration law, which sovereign states have the right to enact—very different from a "right" that would effectively deny sovereignty to another people by moving one's own people into the other's state.

Inevitably, each side sees "return" as an essential component of its national sovereignty. The settlement movement is an expression of my side's right of return to the whole of the land—not only to Haifa but to Hebron. It is the analogue to your side's right of return—not only to Hebron but to Haifa.

To demand a Palestinian right of return to what is now Israel is the political equivalent of Israel demanding the right to continue building settlements in a Palestinian state. It is the "right" to sabotage and destroy the ability of the other side to construct a viable homeland. The practical implementation of partition, then, requires each side to limit its *legitimate* right of return to that part of the land in which each will exercise national sovereignty.

Peace requires a mutual constriction: My side contracts settlements, and your side contracts refugee return. Those reciprocal concessions are the precondition for a two-state solution. My people will fulfill its right of return to the state of Israel, not to the whole land of Israel. Your people will fulfill its right of return to the state of Palestine, not to the whole land of Palestine.

The trade-off, then, is 1948 for 1967. I give up most of the territorial gains of 1967 in exchange for your acceptance of Israel's creation in 1948. And neither side tries to encroach on the sovereignty of the other—not through settlements, not through refugee return.

Palestinian president Mahmoud Abbas almost made that conceptual leap. In 2012, an Israeli reporter asked him what he regards as Palestine. Abbas replied: "Palestine now for me is the '67 borders, with East Jerusalem as its capital. This is now and forever. . . . This is Palestine for me. I am [a] refugee, but I am living in Ramallah."

The interviewer persisted: "Sometimes your official television . . . speak(s) about Acre and Ramle and Jaffa [cities within pre-'67 Israel] as 'Palestine.'"

Abbas: "I believe that [the] West Bank and Gaza is Palestine, and the other parts Israel."

What about the northern Israeli town of Safed, from which Abbas's family fled in 1948?

"It's my right to see it," he said, "but not to live there."

I was galvanized. Suddenly, I no longer felt the paralysis I'd lived with since the second intifada; I allowed myself to once again hope. Here was the moment I'd been waiting for. The conceptual breakthrough. Abbas couldn't have been more explicit, in the most moving personal way. No doublespeak, no subterfuge: 1967 for 1948.

But then, confronted with an outcry among Palestinians, Abbas retracted. I was speaking only as a private individual, said the president of the Palestinian Authority. "No one can give up the right of return."

In fact, each side is guilty of proclaiming its commitment to a two-state solution but proceeding to act in the opposite way. Though every Israeli government in recent years has affirmed a two-state solution, and though there is a long-standing majority of Israelis supporting two states, our side has shown its lack of good faith in the most literal way possible—through concrete and mortar, expanding settlements. And the daily message your society conveys to itself is that a two-state solution is merely a Palestinian tactic on the way to a one-state solution.

In the last two decades, Palestinian leaders have rejected every peace offer in part because of their maximalist interpretation of return. For them, the precondition for peace is my agreement to commit suicide.

I am looking out at Anata, the Shuafat refugee camp, one of the Palestinian villages and neighborhoods within view of my porch. Unlike the refugee camps in Gaza, where Palestinian authorities forbid substantial improvements in living conditions, here at least houses are being built. New apartment buildings loom over the wall. Laundry hangs from some apartments, while others stand empty. Technically a part of municipal Jerusalem, the city's garbage collectors and phone repairmen and firemen are afraid to enter the village. Yet Anata isn't a part of the Palestinian Authority, either. And so its residents live in a kind of no-man's-land, where crime and drugs thrive, casualties of a failed peace process. Still, for all the tragedy of Anata, it is no longer a refugee camp. Anata's residents will not be "returning" anywhere. When a Palestinian state is established, they will almost certainly be among its citizens.

Yet your leaders maintain the fiction of Anata as a refugee camp. One generation after another of

Palestinians is bound to the fantasy of "return" to vanished homes in Israel. The international community is complicit in the deception. In the 1950s, a convergence of interests among the Islamic and Communist and non-aligned blocs led the UN to create UNRWA, United Nations Relief and Works Agency, which funds Palestinian refugee camps, making no distinction between, say, those in Lebanon and those in the West Bank. UNRWA is the only UN organization devoted to a single refugee issue. And Palestinian refugees are the only refugee community in the world whose homeless status is hereditary—even if they live in Palestine. This has resulted in more international funding by far for Palestinian refugees than for any other refugee problem. And what is there to show for it? Only misery and rage.

With the notable exception of Jordan, which granted Palestinian refugees citizenship, the Arab world has kept Palestinians as refugees, stateless and in camps, politicizing their misery as permanent evidence against Israel.

Meanwhile, other humanitarian emergencies demand attention. There are, at last count, some sixty million refugees around the world, many of them from new crises in the Middle East. The special status for Palestinian refugees is unsustainable. And given the certain opposition of any Israeli government to right of return to Israel proper, the issue has become one of the main obstacles to your hopes for national sovereignty.

I know my people: If Israelis sense that peace is possible, there will be a majority to support territorial concessions—just as a majority supported the withdrawal from the Sinai in 1982 and the Oslo peace process in 1993. But to convince Israelis to take frightening security risks in a disintegrating Middle East, we need to hear that the unbearable denial of our right to exist is finally over. We need to hear from our neighbors that Israel is here to stay.

# Isaac and Ishmael

Dear Neighbor,

*Eid mubarak*, a blessed celebration to you. Today is the start of Eid al-Adha, the feast of the sacrifice, marking the Muslim tradition of Abraham's thwarted sacrifice of Ishmael. There is less traffic in my neighborhood; fewer Palestinians from East Jerusalem are riding the light rail. Toward evening, colored lights enliven your hill.

So much entwines Islam and Judaism; so much divides us. We share a common religious sensibility that sees law and spirituality as inseparable, that regulates permitted and forbidden foods to sanctify eating, that abhors graven images as a coarsening of the Divine. Both our faiths have strong mystical traditions, a longing to go beyond faith, to direct encounter with God.

We are religious communities who knew the desert in our formative years and were shaped by the struggle for survival. And, of course, we share a common father, Abraham/Ibrahim, who in both our traditions is the exemplar of hospitality, leaving all sides of his tent open to invite travelers for refreshment.

The other day I went to pray at the Tomb of the Patriarchs and Matriarchs in Hebron. Nowhere in this land do I feel more rooted, and more disoriented, than in this shrine that Muslims call the Ibrahimi Mosque and Jews call the Cave of Machpelah—from the Hebrew word for "doubling," because here are buried the founding couples of the Jewish people: Abraham and Sarah, Isaac and Rebecca, Jacob and Leah. Perhaps *machpelah* hints at another coupling—of Judaism and Islam, the faiths that emerged from Abraham's sons, Isaac and Ishmael. Perhaps, in the Divine plan, we were meant to be entwined, challenged to grow together.

And yet in this place of our shared origin, where Muslims and Jews should recognize each other as inseparable from this land, and Hebrew and Arabic as the languages of its soul—here is where we have most wounded each other.

I began my pilgrimage at an outdoor corner of the massive stone building, whose foundations were laid by the Judean king Herod, over which was built the mosque that stands today. A sign notes that here once stood a staircase where, for centuries, Jews were confined to the seventh step by Muslim authorities, forbidden to enter the building—forbidden to unburden themselves before father Abraham and mother Sarah. Instead, Jews would insert notes with prayers through the cracks of the stones. Recent pilgrims have placed notes in those same cracks, linking their prayers with those of our ancestors who once stood at this place that embodied the humiliation of exile.

I entered the building, divided now between areas for Muslim prayer and Jewish prayer. Once, not so long ago, it was different. In the decades after the Six-Day War, Muslims and Jews would freely mingle here. Muslim women with kerchiefs tied under their chins, and Jewish women with kerchiefs tied behind their necks, silently prayed—if not together, then at least side by side. Watching them in those years, I'd felt that this place assumed an extra dimension of holiness, imparted by the simple act of Muslim and Jewish pilgrims coming together. Yes, it was happening under Israeli army control, and tension was always palpable; but for the first time, we all could gather here, and I felt the blessing of our commingling prayers.

The slender opening that joined our worlds shut

on February 25, 1994, with the Ramadan massacre committed by Baruch Goldstein, a religious Jew, who fired into a crowd of Muslim worshippers in the hall of Isaac and Rebecca, murdering twenty-nine people and wounding dozens more. Acting in the name of God, he committed the ultimate desecration of this sacred place.

I approached the area dedicated to Abraham and Sarah—a small room with high, vaulted ceilings that contains stone cenotaphs marking their graves in the cave below. This is part of the "Jewish" area of the site, and it is separated by a padlocked iron door from the "Muslim" area—where cenotaphs mark the graves below of Rebecca and Isaac. As if either Jews or Muslims could possibly be strangers anywhere in this building.

I sat on a bench against the iron door. This is where the terrorist stood, calmly loading and reloading his automatic weapon as he fired into crowds of men and women bent in prayer. How could you? I asked him. How dare you desecrate the name of God and your people?

The muezzin's call to prayer filled the building. The voice was so strong, it seemed to be coming from the walls. I noticed some Jews turning visibly anxious. But one young man in a black hat and side locks, a visitor from New York, said to me, "You know, when you think about what they're saying—'*Allahu akbar*,' God is great—it's a good thing, no?" Yes: so obvious, and yet in Hebron, Muslims and Jews can never take each other's goodwill for granted. I wanted to hug him.

Our conflict, neighbor, isn't merely a national or territorial dispute but has assumed transcendent dimensions, touching on the deepest fears and hopes of Muslims and Jews. This immeasurably complicates our chances for a solution. And it is poisoning Muslim–Jewish relations around the world. That places an added responsibility on us to try to defuse the emotions roused on both sides by our conflict.

But how to respect the other's religious commitments and longings when those seem to threaten our own? That wrenching dilemma is especially acute regarding the status of the holy places we share—and none more so than the Temple Mount, the Haram el Sharif, spiritual and emotional center point of our conflict.

Many Jews fail to understand the depth of the Muslim connection with the Mount's Al-Aqsa Mosque, where worshippers come to experience the tangible presence of the Prophet who, you believe, ascended from there to Heaven, rupturing the barrier separating this world from the next. I often encounter, especially from Jews on the right, a dismissal of the significance of the Mount for Muslims. It's "only" Islam's third-holiest site, some will say, as though holiness could be quantified. (The Machpelah is "only" the second-holiest site in Judaism, and yet its significance for religious Jews—and its historical significance for many secular Jews—is immeasurable.)

We Israelis also need to understand how the Mount has become a symbol for Muslims of occupation. The fact that you, neighbor, cannot freely cross the wall and pray in Al-Aqsa without a security permit is an ongoing wound, one that is at once political and spiritual. Israelis need to recognize the deep pain we've caused in pursuing our security needs.

In the Muslim–Jewish conversation about our shared holy sites, we desperately need a discourse of spiritual dignity, not a discourse that disgraces the very holiness we seek to uphold.

Many non-Jews believe that our holiest site is the Western Wall. In fact, that is merely part of the retaining wall that once surrounded the Temple. For Jews, the Temple Mount is our holiest place, the literal center point of creation. Here, we believe, God's Presence came to dwell among the people of Israel. Jews mourn the loss of the Temple not only as the end of our national sovereignty and the beginning of our exile from the land but, more deeply, the "exile" of the tangible Divine Presence from our midst. The deep connection we've maintained with the Temple Mount is, in part, our refusal to accept that exile as the final word. No matter where a Jew is in the world, he or she will turn in prayer toward the Temple Mount.

The biblical prophecy is that, in the end of days, the nations will gather in pilgrimage to the Mount, and God's House will be "a House of Prayer for all people." I don't know how that will happen. Nor is it my religious obligation as a Jew to plan that moment. There is a wise rabbinic parable about how the future Temple will appear: in a cloud of fire, descending from Heaven. The parable is a warning, especially to Jews today who once again control Jerusalem: Rebuilding the Temple is not in your hands. Leave the Mount to God.

And so, while I cannot relinquish my claim to the Temple Mount without doing violence to a core vision of Judaism, I do relinquish its realization through human hands.

But I need your side, neighbor, to reconsider some of its positions, too. I need your leaders to end their campaign denying any Jewish connection to the holy places. The relentless message from Palestinian media is that there was no ancient Temple in Jerusalem, no

Jewish attachment to the Western Wall, no archaeological proof of Jewish roots in this land at all. When
Palestinian Authority president Abbas would speak
of Jerusalem, he'd invoke the Muslim and Christian
historical presence and pointedly omit the Jewish
presence.

Every Palestinian leader, religious or political, with
whom I've spoken over the years has insisted that, under a Palestinian state, Jews would have no right to
pray at the Machpelah, that Jews have no attachment
to the site, which can function only as a mosque. Jews
would be welcome to visit, Palestinian leaders said to
me—but as tourists, not pilgrims. For Jews, that would
be the modern equivalent of the seventh step.

I am left emotionally paralyzed before this systematic denial of my connection to the holiest places in
Judaism. How to respond? By citing the Israeli mu-
seums that are filled with archaeological proof of my
history here? Or the accounts of travelers to Jerusalem
through the centuries? Or—to say nothing at all, because even entering into a debate somehow legitimizes
the assault?

Then there is the relentless accusation from Palestinian leaders of a threat to Al-Aqsa. In recent years
Jews have been targeted by a wave of terror attacks—
stabbings and shootings and car rammings—all in the

name of "saving" Al-Aqsa from a supposed Israeli government plot to undermine and ultimately destroy the Muslim presence on the Mount.

I tell you, neighbor, with all urgency: There is no government plot to destroy Al-Aqsa or in any way lessen the Muslim presence on the Mount. The notion of a Jewish plot against Al-Aqsa is a baseless rumor that has been spread, in one form or another, since the 1920s, often with disastrous results, encouraging murder in the name of God. (The 1929 massacre in Hebron was a result of that poisoned rumor.) Israeli policy since the Six-Day War has been to accommodate the Muslim presence and restrain the Jewish presence, going so far as to forbid Jewish prayer.

When Israeli paratroopers reached the Temple Mount on the morning of June 7, 1967, their first impulse was to reclaim the site for the Jewish people. And so two paratroopers climbed up the Dome of the Rock and hoisted an Israeli flag. Defense Minister Moshe Dayan, who was watching through binoculars from nearby Mount Scopus, radioed the paratroopers' commander and ordered the flag immediately removed. It is, in retrospect, an astonishing example of restraint. The Jewish people had just returned to its holiest site, to which we had been denied access for centuries, only to effectively yield sovereignty at this moment of triumph. Shortly after the war, Dayan met with Muslim officials and formally granted them veto power over the right to pray on the Mount.

Most religious Jews accept that arrangement. In fact, most won't even walk on the Temple Mount, fearful of transgressing on the Holy of Holies, the Temple's inner sanctum, whose exact location is no longer known. Yes, there is a growing movement— fortunately still fringe—to pressure the Israeli government to change the status quo by allowing Jewish prayer on the Mount. But mainstream Israel is restraining that dangerous longing. Even right-wing Israeli governments have upheld this policy.

I understand those of my fellow Jews who find the situation absurd. And frankly, it is absurd. When Jews go up to the Temple Mount, they are "escorted" by Muslim officials who watch their lips to ensure that no prayers are being silently said. Violators are hauled away and arrested—by Israeli police. For a Jew to be prevented—by a Jewish government—from praying there of all places?

And yet, like most Israelis, I accept the restriction we've imposed on ourselves. Certainly, in forbidding Jewish prayer on the Temple Mount, the Israeli government is acting out of pragmatic rather than altruistic considerations, seeking to prevent a religious war.

Still, pragmatism, especially over religious claims, is a precious rarity in our part of the world. And has there ever been an example, in the history of religion, of such restraint regarding a people's holiest place?

Ultimately, peace is about mutual respect. Israelis need to treat Palestinians with dignity. The truth is that, for many Israeli Jews, treating others with respect can be a challenge. Israel is a restless society of up-rooted and re-rooted refugees and children of refugees, and the dark side of our vitality is a frankness that can easily become rudeness, the antithesis of Arab decorousness. Israelis often don't know how to treat each other with respect, let alone those we are occupying. We are a people in a hurry to compensate for our lost centuries of nationhood, a people that doesn't pay attention to niceties. Sometimes I think that, if only we'd known how to show your people simple respect, so much could have been different here.

What I need from you is respect for my people's story. The campaign against our connection to this land and its holy sites tells Jews that our conflict isn't about occupation or settlements but is, instead, a war against Jewish history. The attempt to erase us conceptually, many Jews fear, is a first step toward erasing us physically.

Each side needs to confront the psychological impact

of our offenses against the other. We must recognize the ways in which we are, for each other, embodiments of our greatest fears, and learn to respect each other's difficult histories. My side needs to stop reinforcing the Muslim trauma of colonialism, and your side, the Jewish trauma of destruction. As long as our conflict remains a focus for the wounds of the Muslim and Jewish past, peace will continue to elude us.

Does religion doom us to endless conflict? Judaism versus Islam? One sacred claim against another?

I believe that our faiths contain resources to help us live in peace and dignity as neighbors. But we need to frankly concede that each faith also contains obstacles to compromise. Can Judaism accept partition of land it considers sacred, a Divine trust given to the people of Israel, and come to terms with the counterclaim of another people? Can Islam accept the legitimacy of a Jewish-majority state located in the Muslim world, accept Jews not only as *dhimmi*, "protected people" relegated to secondary status under Islam, but as equals entitled to national sovereignty?

Our Scriptures offer complicated portraits of each other. The Qur'an and the Hadith describe Jews as sinners and ingrates, but also, along with Christians, as a "people of the Book" deserving respect. The Torah and rabbinic commentators portray Ishmael—and implicitly through him the Arab and Muslim peoples—as violent and coarse, but also as a recipient of Divine blessing. The archetypes in both traditions are hardly flattering—yet they also contain a basis for respecting the other's spiritual dignity.

We need to seek out those generous voices embedded in our traditions and offer new interpretations of old concepts—which is, after all, how religions cope with change. Our traditions invite interpretation. That very flexibility helped Judaism survive. Religion can be a force for endless conflict or for peaceful resolution. In part that depends on how we choose to read our sacred texts. Islam and Judaism are rich and complicated worlds. We carry the light but also the weight of centuries. Each tradition must grapple with its own challenges.

From my side, the message of the Torah would appear to be unequivocal: God has given this land to the people of Israel. For some Jews, that is the final word on the matter: We are its rightful possessors and there is nothing more to discuss. Certainly not sharing the land with a counterclaimant—with you. That is how the settlement movement understands the question of ownership of the land. In this view there is no room for your national claims.

I would like to suggest another religious way of reading this story.

Built into the Jewish relationship to the land of Israel is the commandment to periodically relinquish ownership. Every seven years the land is to be laid fallow, returned to its pristine state. And on the fiftieth year all ownership and debts are to be forfeited. The fruit of new trees cannot be eaten for the first three years; the corners of one's field must be left for the poor. Those agricultural commandments apply only to the land of Israel.

The message is that a holy land doesn't belong to us but to God. The elusiveness of possession is an expression of the land's holiness. The sacred can never be fully owned by mortal beings. Sacred space is an encounter with a world beyond boundaries, a dimension in which all human claims are irrelevant.

Does God want us to exclusively possess the land? Or are we meant in this time to share it with another people? For me the very conditionality of ownership, the fact that no one and no people can really own holy land, offers a religious basis for sharing the land between us. As custodians, not owners.

The religious Israeli voices I find most compelling are those that are faithful to the terms of conditional ownership. There have been leading Israeli rabbis who painfully concluded that the price was too high for fulfilling our claim to the entirety of the land. Some moderate rabbis argue that the holiness of life—the need to prevent bloodshed—supersedes the holiness of the land. Still others recall the verse by Isaiah: "Zion will be redeemed through justice." In this reading of my tradition, being faithful to the land means being prepared to relinquish our exclusive hold on it.

When I went on my journey through Palestinian Islam before the second intifada, I befriended a Sufi sheikh I'll call Ibrahim. Sheikh Ibrahim took me to mosques around the country; under his spiritual protection, I felt safe to go anywhere. What drew us together was a kind of holy curiosity of the other's world, a delight in our differences as much as in our commonalities. He quoted the powerful Qur'anic verse: "O people! Behold, We have created you all out of a male and a female, and have made you into nations and tribes, so that you might come to know one another." Eyes widening, the sheikh exclaimed: "What does it say? To kill each other? No! To know each other! What does my brother Yossi Halevi know? He is a religious person; what is his wisdom? Who is Ibrahim, and what does he have to teach Yossi Halevi? What did God create in you that He didn't create in me?"

I asked the sheikh about the conflicting versions in our respective traditions of the story of Abraham's sacrifice of his son. To whom does this story belong? In our current war over competing national and religious narratives, are Palestinians and Israelis playing out an ancient rivalry between Abraham's two sons?

Sheikh Ibrahim dismissed my concern. "There is no problem! What was Ishmael's greatness? What was Isaac's greatness? That they accepted whatever God wanted. I wish for Yossi Halevi's children, for Ibrahim's children, to be like Isaac and Ishmael." What the sheikh was telling me was, Don't focus on the conflicting details but on the unifying message in the two narratives. Let it be Isaac, let it be Ishmael, or better yet, let it be both. There was room enough on the altar for all those Muslims and Jews who loved God and were willing to sacrifice for the Divine will.

Each of our religious traditions has tried to stay faithful to its founding stories. For Muslims that means surrendering to God to fulfill human destiny. For Jews, it means partnering with God to help heal a wounded world.

The difference in those two approaches is manifest in how each of our Scriptures tells the story of Abraham confronting the imminent destruction of Sodom. In the Torah, Abraham negotiates with God: If there are fifty righteous people in Sodom, will You spare the sinful city? How about forty? Thirty? Ten? God seems to encourage Abraham's desperate bid, a rebellion against Heaven for the sake of Heaven.

In the Qur'an, too, Ibrahim initially challenges God's decision to destroy the city. But he is quickly silenced. Who are you, a mere mortal, God says, to question My ways? Ibrahim acquiesces, surrenders to what he cannot understand.

Both stories offer models of the Divine-human interaction and tell us something essential about the differences between our two faiths—differences I celebrate. I cherish the holy chutzpah of the Torah's Abraham, who cannot abide suffering, even when Divinely initiated. That restless spirit is embodied in the Jewish study hall, where questions are no less important than answers and where one is encouraged to argue with the tradition.

And I cherish the wise surrender of the Qur'an's Ibrahim, whose humility acknowledges the ultimate futility of human ideas and ambitions. That humility is played out on the Muslim prayer mat, offering the totality of oneself in prostration before God.

Each faith, of course, has known both surrender and rigorous inquiry. In Judaism, there is a long and powerful tradition of martyrdom dating back to pagan times, of faithful Jews preferring death to forcible conversion. Jewish history has repeatedly generated movements of spiritual renewal, emphasizing devotion and surrender to God's will.

And in Islam you have the great tradition of philosophical and scientific inquiry that influenced the Renaissance and transformed humanity.

Today, though, each faith community suffers from a decline of one or the other aspect of religious vitality. Modernity has not been kind to Jewish spirituality: Large parts of the Jewish people have become severed from basic faith and devotion. The Muslim world has the opposite problem: an erosion of open inquiry and self-critique.

Perhaps we can help restore each other to balance. Jews, I feel, need something of the Muslim prayer mat; my Muslim friends say they need something of the Jewish study hall. Can we inspire each other to renew our spiritual greatness?

Both our peoples are warm and generous—among ourselves. But we show our hardest face toward each other. Instead, we need to draw on the deep resources of our faith and see ourselves as inseparable parts of a shared sacred story.

That shared story begins with our father Abraham/

Ibrahim's revolt against idolatry, smashing his father's graven images and proclaiming the oneness of God— and through that radical insight, the oneness of humanity. In cherishing the legacy of our shared father, we partake of that seminal moment of the birth of a new human consciousness. And we share the longing for a world liberated from idolatry in all its forms, from all that clouds our perception of divine reality.

Both our traditions note that Abraham/Ibrahim was buried by Isaac and Ishmael, who overcame their rivalry to honor their father. Along with conflict, that, too, is our legacy. So is our father's generosity: Perhaps the memory of his hospitality can help us find a way to accommodate each other's presence in this land.

# The Israeli Paradox

Dear Neighbor,

In the days before the suicide bombings of the early 2000s, before the wall was built, Palestinians and Israelis had opportunities to get to know each other. The occupation, of course, always stood between us. Still, there was human interaction.

But now we've become abstractions to each other. What worries me about the next generation is that even limited encounters between our peoples are increasingly rare. On both sides, rage and hatred are growing among our young people. Any possibility for coexistence depends on each side having at least some positive interaction, some knowledge of the other's reality.

I have already told you something of my faith, my

personal history, and the story of my people. Now, in the spirit of the Qur'an's exhortation to know each other, I'd like to tell you something about modern-day Israel, the society that exists within plain view from your hill—who we are and how we manage our internal issues. After all, our two nations are bound to each other. How my country works will have implications for both our futures.

If I had to sum up in one word what most characterizes Israeli society, it is: paradox.

Our Declaration of Independence defined Israel as a Jewish and a democratic state. According to the framers, Israel would be the homeland of Jews around the world, whether or not they are Israeli citizens. And it would be the democratic state of all its citizens, whether or not they are Jews. That dual identity—Jewish and democratic—is the aspirational challenge bequeathed to us by the founders.

Is Israel a secular or a religious state? Partly that depends on where the question is being asked. Seen from Tel Aviv, with its clubs and nonkosher restaurants, Israel is a thoroughly secular society. Seen from Jerusalem, with its synagogues and study halls, Israel is a deeply traditional society. I define Israel as a secular state in a holy land. When Zionism determined that there could be no substitute national home for the Jews but Zion, it ensured a permanent conflict between religion and state that can only be managed, never entirely resolved.

Israel is an uneasy meeting point between Jews from East and West. For Mizrahim, or Jews from Muslim countries, that encounter often meant, especially in Israel's early years, discrimination and patronizing contempt from the Ashkenazi European establishment; today, increasingly, the encounter between Ashkenazim and Mizrahim happens under the wedding canopy. The core community that founded Israel was overwhelmingly Ashkenazi and secular, and secularism remains vibrant; at the same time our music, cuisine, even language are all increasingly influenced by traditional Mizrahi culture. The oud has met the electric guitar: *Piyutim*, the prayer poems of Mizrahim, have been retrieved from the cultural amnesia of secular Israel and adopted by our leading rock musicians. Israeli music was once the carrier of the secular ethos; today it expresses the longing among Israelis to reconnect with Jewish tradition.

I know Israeli Jews of Middle Eastern origin whose passion for Oum Kalthoum, the great Egyptian singer, is part of their family identity. And there are Israeli singers and bands—like Orphaned Land, which combines heavy metal with *piyut*—that are popular in Arab and Muslim countries. When the band performs in Turkey—the only Muslim country that has allowed them to appear—fans from Lebanon and Egypt and even Iran come, some waving their national flags.

Recently I attended a concert celebrating both Jewish and Arab music, held outside the walls of Jerusalem's Old City. The concert drew not only Israeli Jews but Palestinians from the Old City and elsewhere in Jerusalem. Onstage were Jews singing in Arabic and Arabs singing in Hebrew. Peace isn't just a political but a cultural challenge. The more Israel reclaims its Eastern identity, the better the chance of finding our place in the region.

Paradox is built into the very nature of Israeli society, created by the "ingathering of the exiles," as we call the immigration of Jews from around the world. Jews brought home the wisdom and fears learned from their varied wanderings and imposed those on Israeli reality. As a Jew raised in New York in the 1960s who absorbed the pluralistic values of American society, I came to Israel with a commitment to help strengthen its democratic culture. I fear the weakening of democratic norms, especially among young Israelis, who grew up after the collapse of the peace process and whose formative memories have been terrorism and rocket assaults from Lebanon and Gaza. I was grateful to the IDF for putting on trial an Israeli soldier who shot and killed a disarmed Palestinian assailant in Hebron. Yet even though the soldier had violated the Israeli army's code of ethics and rules of engagement, many celebrated him as a hero.

But I know Israelis from the former Soviet Union, for example, who grew up as an oppressed minority under a totalitarian regime. Their great anxiety is that the Jews, so long defenseless, have yet to learn how to effectively wield power. They worry that democratic niceties, like an army code of ethics, are a luxury that a besieged country cannot afford, and that those self-imposed restraints undermine our ability to defend ourselves.

It often seems to me that the Israeli national debate is really Jewish history arguing with itself. Who are we? What does our history expect of us? How do we reconcile, or simply live with, our multiple paradoxes?

Inevitably, Israel reflects the contradictions of the Jews. We came home with opposite expectations of what a Jewish state should be. Secular Zionists longed for a state that would "normalize" the Jews, one of history's most abnormal peoples, by creating a nation among nations. In the process of demythologizing the

Jewish people, secularists hoped that anti-Semitism would gradually disappear.

Religious Zionists, on the other hand, longed for a state that would confirm Jewish exceptionalism, become a "light to the nations," even a trigger for the redemption of humanity. How the Jewish state could be both normal and exceptional was a dilemma that remained abstract for the Zionist movement—until we actually achieved statehood. Now contradictory visions have become social conflicts.

There is a seminal moment in the Bible, when the elders of Israel approach Samuel the prophet (whose grave, not far from our two hills, is located in a building that peacefully contains both a mosque and a synagogue). The elders demand that Samuel anoint a king over Israel, so that we will be "like all the nations." Normal: freed of the burden of chosenness. Samuel is outraged. Israel is governed by prophets; why would the elders want a mere king as ruler?

Those impulses—to be normal and to be exceptional—are the twin longings that run through Jewish history. Zionism's genius—and one of the reasons for its success among the world's Jews—was that it embraced those two longings and promised the Jews to fulfill them both.

I share those contradictory longings. I see the

transformation of the Jews back into a sovereign nation as one of the great achievements of Jewish history. I want Israel to be normal, accepted by the international community, more at home in its ordinariness, able to finally take existence for granted. But I also want an Israel that seeks more than existence, that cherishes the vision of the prophets of a just society—that is worthy of all the hopes and prayers and efforts invested in its founding.

Ironically, we have yet to truly fulfill either vision, of normalcy or exceptionalism. Israel is a nation-state, but hardly normal. We are often the great exception, the outcast—from the Middle East, from the UN. As for the wish to be an exemplary society, Israel often feels painfully normal, with political corruption and organized crime and all the ailments of modernity. The founders sought to create a nation that would be normalized in its relations with the world but internally exceptional, a laboratory of democratic socialism. Sometimes, though, it seems as if we've created the reverse dynamic: externally abnormal, internally unexceptional.

Perhaps this is Israel's greatest challenge: to become a normal nation among nations while aspiring to create a society worthy of Jewish history and dreams. One reason I am reaching out to you, neighbor, is that

Israel's ability to fulfill both those aspirations will depend, in part, on our relationship with you and your people.

Secular and religious Israelis are still arguing about normalcy and exceptionalism. Neither is likely to entirely prevail, because both arguments speak to an essential Jewish need. After the Holocaust, even many religious Jews agreed that secular Zionism's promise of normalization offered vital healing for the Jewish people. And today, with growing materialism in our society, many secular Jews agree that Israeli society needs an infusion of spirituality, a renewed sense of purpose and direction.

I live at the uneasy meeting point between tradition and modernity. I am a religious Jew, but I don't vote for a religious party. I want to keep religion as far away from politics as possible. At the same time, I recognize that this isn't America, and that in our region, and in a Jewish-majority country, there cannot be complete separation between religion and state. I once interviewed one of the leaders of secular revolt against the rabbinic establishment, and I assumed that her model for Israel was the American separation of religion and state. But she surprised me: That's impossible in Israel, she said. Religion is too much a part of the nation's identity.

And yet secularism is also an essential part of our identity. Because of the centrality of peoplehood for Judaism, the most strictly observant Jews have no choice but to accept the most secular as fellow Jews. And so Israel must accommodate religious and secular, ensuring that both see a reflection of their identities in the national ethos.

To ease religious–secular tensions, we have reached a series of compromises. The Orthodox-run state rabbinate, for example, has a monopoly on marriage—a carry-over from the Ottoman Empire, where every religion had its own courts for personal status issues. (Sharia courts have the same legal status in Israel as rabbinic courts.) That means that there is no option of civil marriage in Israel, for either Jews or Muslims. But if a couple flies, say, to Cyprus, twenty minutes away, and gets married in a civil court, their marriage will be recognized by the state when they return home.

Sooner or later this absurd system will have to change, if only because more and more young Israeli Jews are opting out, choosing to fly abroad and marry without an Orthodox rabbi.

Then there's the compromise over public observance of the Sabbath. One of the first questions that vexed Israel after its founding was, How should a modern Jewish state observe Shabbat in its public space?

Should it forbid activities considered violations of the Sabbath under Orthodox law, or treat the day as any other?

Israel opted, as usual, for a messy compromise. Public transportation is suspended on Shabbat in Jewish areas and commerce more or less banned, but cultural and sports events are permitted, and restaurants and cafés remain open. In recent years the so-called status quo on Shabbat observance has been eroded, and commerce on Shabbat has expanded. One possible update to the status quo, jointly presented by a leading rabbi and a leading secular jurist, would permit limited public transportation and maintain entertainment while enforcing the ban on commerce, which is the most blatant violation of the spirit of Shabbat. In that way, each Israeli Jew could determine his or her way of enjoying the day of rest. That suggested compromise is an example of religious–secular relations at their best: figuring out how to make a place in our public space for a range of approaches to Jewish tradition.

Israel was founded by secular Jews—many of them in revolt against their religious families—and so secularism is built into our foundations. It is also the safety net against rising fundamentalism. But like most Israeli Jews, I want Jewish values and culture to shape our public space. (What constitutes "Jewish values" is part of the ongoing debate over our identity.) Polls show that a majority of Jewish citizens want less religious legislation and more tradition in their lives. I believe that that is where Israel is ultimately heading. It's a delicate balance between our secular and religious identities, and each generation will need to renegotiate the details. The premise of all those arrangements must continue to be that no part of Israeli society be allowed to totally determine the face of Israeli culture and politics.

To further complicate matters, there is the ongoing feud between the Israeli government and the Reform and Conservative Jewish denominations over who has the right to control prayer at the Western Wall. A government compromise that would have granted official status to those liberal denominations over one area of the Wall collapsed following the opposition of ultra-Orthodox parties, who oppose recognition of the non-Orthodox movements. Given that a majority of American Jews who practice Judaism identify either as Reform or Conservative, the crisis has created a rupture between Israel and the Diaspora.

I find the anger and anguish of Reform and Conservative Jews deeply moving. What they're saying to Israel in effect is: You are supposed to be the homeland of all Jews, which means your public space needs to reflect our religious diversity; by granting exclusive control to one part of the Jewish people, the Orthodox, you are betraying the Zionist commitment to peoplehood.

Not only does Israel have to manage its radical Jewish diversity; its even greater challenge is including Arab citizens—fully 20 percent of the population, many of whom identify as Palestinian—in its national identity.

Israel must honor its two nonnegotiable identities, as a Jewish state and a democratic state. Israel cannot give up its commitment to being the continuation of Jewish history and the potential protector of the world's Jews without doing irreparable damage to its essence. So much of Israel's vitality and achievements comes from the country's Jewish identity, from the motivation to turn a two-thousand-year dream into an ongoing miracle of fulfillment. Remove the Jewishness of Israel—and its heart, its passion are excised.

But failure to embrace Arab citizens in the national identity and public space creates a different kind of existential threat. I once asked an Arab Knesset member what his most "Israeli" moment was. I expected him to mention his swearing-in as a member of parliament, or perhaps his pride over the victory of an Israeli sports team. Instead he said: I never had an Israeli moment; I've never once felt Israeli.

For Israel's Arab citizens, the problem of their identity is embodied in Israel's national anthem, which evokes the Jewish longing for Zion. "So long as the Jewish soul yearns within the heart," it begins. As one Arab Israeli said to me: I have no problem with a Jewish heart, I just don't have one. An Arab Supreme Court justice, who presided over the sentencing to prison of a former Israeli president (on charges of rape)—surely an expression of a judge's unassailable status in society—told an interviewer that he doesn't sing the national anthem.

How do Jewish Israelis and Arab Israelis celebrate Independence Day together, when for Jews it is a day of redemption and for Palestinians a day of catastrophe?

Fully opening up Israeli identity to Palestinian Israelis is a frightening prospect for both Arabs and Jews. For Arabs it means taking an active role in the public life of a nation that is occupying their relatives in the West Bank. For Jews it means trusting as fellow citizens a population whose natural sympathy may be with the Palestinians and the Arab world, with the country's enemies.

Can there be a more paradoxical identity, given our situation, than "Palestinian Israeli"? During the

2006 war between Israel and the Lebanese Islamist Hezbollah, I was in an Arab restaurant in the northern city of Haifa when the siren went off, warning of an imminent missile attack. Arabs and Jews all crowded for shelter in the kitchen. We stood pressed together in awkward silence. Finally, someone said, "Coexistence." Everyone smiled ruefully. The surreal moment caught the paradox of Israeli Palestinians: seeking shelter together with Jews from a missile attack launched in the name of the Palestinian cause.

And yet, for all the awkwardness and ambivalence and anger, I believe that a sense of shared citizenship between Israeli Jews and Arabs isn't just essential but also possible. Polls consistently show that a majority of Arab Israelis believe that Israel is a good country to live in, even though half also say that Arabs are discriminated against; even more surprising, a majority say they are proud to be Israeli. Asked whether they would opt for citizenship in a future Palestinian state, the overwhelming majority say no, even if they could remain in their homes and not move across the border.

The bad news for my country is that a large minority of Arabs is alienated from Israeli society. Some Palestinian Israelis don't call themselves Israeli at all, preferring the term "Palestinians of 1948"—that is, Palestinians who didn't leave during the Nakba.

Yet the fact that a majority of Palestinian citizens of Israel still identify to some extent with the state, even with no end in sight for our conflict, means that there is a basis from which to work toward a shared society and identity, however fraught. As a citizen of Israel, I am committed to this effort.

How, then, to proceed? Mohammad Darawshe, one of the leading Palestinian Israeli activists and my colleague at the Hartman Institute, says that Israel's Arabs need to learn to act like a minority and Israel's Jews need to learn to act like a majority. He has, I believe, touched on the psychological core of the problem.

Israel's Jews are a curious majority: We are a majority in our own country but are acutely aware of being a minority in a hostile region—a region to which Arab Israelis belong, by culture and sentiment. That means that both the Jews and the Arabs of Israel often feel at once like a majority and a minority.

Darawshe's challenge to Jews is to remember that we are, after all, in control of a powerful and successful country, and we must act with the generosity of a self-confident majority. His challenge to Arabs is to act with the wisdom of a minority caught in an extremely delicate situation, between their loyalty to their Palestinian identity and the need to find their place in a Jewish-majority society.

Many Jews fear Arab citizens as a potential fifth column. Those fears are reinforced by Arab Knesset members, some of whom openly identify, even during wartime, with Israel's enemies, like Hamas and Hezbollah. Arab parliamentarians have called Israeli soldiers Nazis and supported terror attacks. One Arab MK refused to call the kidnapping of three Israeli teenagers (who were later found murdered) an act of terror. Those are not isolated incidents but part of a pattern.

As the majority, Jews need to reassure Arab citizens that we see them as an integral part of our society. The first place to begin is by ending discrimination against Arab citizens, especially in government allocations for education and infrastructure and other needs. That disgrace violates the promise of Israel's founders to create a society in the spirit of prophetic justice. In some ways the situation is gradually improving—and even the right-wing Netanyahu government invested significant resources in the Arab community, realizing that the Israeli economy will suffer if a substantial part of the population remains behind. But in other ways we are moving backward—like the plethora of laws, proposed by right-wing legislators, emphasizing the Jewishness of the state at the expense of its democratic identity. While few of those laws actually pass, they are creating a mood in which democracy is on the defensive.

As part of the regional majority, Israel's Arabs need to reassure Jewish citizens that they want to be part of Israel—beginning with electing Knesset members whose goal is integrationist, rather than nationalist or Islamist. The gap between the polls that show an appreciation of Israel among Arab citizens with the expressions of alienation and even hatred by Knesset members representing them is untenable. It only reinforces the darkest fears of Israeli Jews.

So long as our conflict persists, relations between Arabs and Jews in Israel will remain abnormal. At the very least, though, Israeli Jews need to convey to Israeli Arabs that we see their place in our society not as a problem to be managed but as an opportunity for Israel to uphold its own moral standards. And by integrating Arabs into Israeli identity, we are taking a step toward integrating Israel into the region.

In the end, I don't know if our internal paradoxes can be resolved. Nor perhaps should they be: Any attempt to embrace one definition of Israel at the exclusion of another will alienate major segments of the population from the national ethos and do violence to the delicate balance that manages our conflicting identities and longings.

At its best, Israel is energized by paradox. I see Israel as a testing ground for managing some of the world's most acute dilemmas—the clash between religion and modernity, East and West, ethnicity and democracy, security and morality. These are worthy challenges for an ancient people that wandered the world and absorbed its diversity—and has brought the world with it back home.

In fact, the balance between our paradoxes is constantly shifting. Few societies are as malleable, so prone to fundamental change in so short a time, as Israel.

In my nearly four decades here, I've lived through at least three distinct Israels. There was the depressed Israel of the 1980s—300 percent inflation, a no-win war in Lebanon, increasing isolation from the international community. Then there was the exuberant Israel of the early 1990s—the Oslo process, the beginning of high-tech start-up Israel, massive immigration from the former Soviet Union, increasing acceptance by the international community. And then there was the Israel that emerged with the collapse of the peace process in the year 2000—moving from one war to the next, its civilian population the target of suicide bombers and rockets, a dreamless Israel living one day at a time, that never lowers its guard.

This Israel has persisted now for nearly two decades. But if the past is any indication, we are due for another drastic shift in the Israeli story. My hope, neighbor, is that, at the next turn, our two societies will renew their encounter, but this time on the basis of mutual respect.

## Victims and Survivors

Dear Neighbor,

Today at 11:00 a.m. the siren sounded for Holocaust Memorial Day. On my hill everything came to a standstill for two full minutes. Drivers pulled to the side of the road and stood in silence. Schools, factories, offices, army bases: all activity suspended. An entire people at one with its wound.

And then I thought of you. No doubt you heard the siren on your hill, too. What were you thinking? Did you feel a sense of human solidarity with us? Or was this a moment of bitter irony for you: the occupier flaunting old wounds, pretending to still be the victim?

Until now I've avoided writing to you about the Holocaust. The omission was deliberate. Its weight can overwhelm us both. And it's too easy to manipulate:

Against you—as dismissive of your suffering (because how can occupation compare to *that*?). And against me—as indictment (because how can Jews of all people mistreat others after what was done to them?).

Finally, I wanted to tell a narrative of the Jewish people's return to this land that didn't reinforce the assumption I've heard for decades from Palestinians and from Muslims generally: that the only reason Israel exists is Western guilt over the Holocaust. Israelis were appalled when President Barack Obama, in addressing the Muslim world in his 2009 Cairo speech, could offer no justification for Israel's existence other than the Holocaust. Obama meant well; his intention was to challenge the Holocaust denial widespread in the Muslim world. But that's not what Israelis heard. What about our four-thousand-year connection to the land? Israelis demanded. What about our story?

(President Obama later tried to correct that misstep, pointedly noting during a visit to the Yad Vashem Holocaust memorial in Jerusalem that Israel's legitimacy is based not on Jewish suffering but on Jewish faith and attachment to the land.)

I recently came across this anonymous message on Facebook: "The rebirth of Israel didn't occur because of the Holocaust. The Holocaust occurred because there was no Israel."

Confronting the Holocaust in our conversation is as unavoidable as that haunting siren. Even as the last of the survivors die out, the Holocaust continues to shape our conflict, in obvious and subtle ways. And so, neighbor, let me try to explain what happens on my hill, among my people, when the siren sounds, and how the Holocaust affects how we think of you and our conflict.

Last night I went to the official ceremony, held at Yad Vashem. Israel's president, Reuven Rivlin, spoke about the need for Jews to free themselves of Holocaust trauma: "The Jewish people was not born in Auschwitz," he said. "It was not fear that kept us going through two thousand years of exile, it was our spiritual assets, our shared creativity, . . . The Holocaust is permanently branded in our flesh. . . . Still, the Holocaust is not the lens through which we should examine our past and our future." Rivlin also warned Jews against misusing Holocaust memory to score political points, even against our enemies. Courageously, Rivlin condemned his political mentor, former prime minister Menachem Begin, for declaring Israel's 1982 invasion of Lebanon an attempt to preempt another Holocaust.

Six survivors then lit torches, each in memory of a million victims. There was the Ukrainian partisan with a chest full of Soviet medals, the Algerian-born woman who survived hiding in Paris. Each told his or her story. They spoke of their wartime suffering matter-of-factly; but they were clearly proud of the lives they'd created after the war, of their children and grandchildren. In turning from victims into survivors, they had extracted destiny from mere fate. Most of all, they spoke of their love for and gratitude to Israel, which allowed them to heal.

For me, as the son of a survivor, what is ultimately most significant about the Holocaust is that we survived it, not as victims but as victors. We are a people long practiced in endurance. We have outlived the empires that tried to destroy us—going back to ancient Egypt and Babylon and Rome. But in our long and improbable history, nothing can quite compare to the resurrection Jews managed in the twentieth century. It's as if all that came before was mere prelude, practice for the moment when Jews had to choose between continuity and extinction.

My father survived the war in a hole in the forest. When the Jews of his town were ghettoized, as the final stage before deportation to Auschwitz, he escaped with two friends. A forest keeper, who'd once worked for my grandfather, an owner of vineyards, occasionally brought food to the three young men.

In 1945, when the war ended, my father returned home and found a Jewish wasteland. Together with the few young Jews who began trickling back from the death camps, he spent those first weeks of freedom drinking. And then, one day, he stirred himself from numbness. He told me that his parents, who had been killed in Auschwitz, had appeared to him—half dream, half vision—and he took their stern gaze as a rebuke against self-pity.

I am the son not of destruction but of rebirth. And so, on this day, I think not only of the fact that I carry the name of my grandfather who died in a gas chamber but that my son carries the name of his grandfather—my father—who survived.

I remain in permanent astonishment about the Holocaust. The industrialization of mass murder. The creation of factories to produce corpses (the endpoint of soulless modernity). The meticulous planning by government and corporate bureaucrats. (What gas will be most effective? What is the best delivery system?) The elaborate ruses devised to lull the victims about their final destination. This was no outburst of hate or vengeance, no mere pogrom, but the ultimate premeditated crime, a crime of dispassion. And it went on, unimpeded, for nearly six years.

Sometimes I find myself unconsciously thinking,

Did it really happen? Could it have happened? My bewilderment surprises me: I have, after all, been struggling with this history all my life. At those moments, I realize that a part of me remains inconsolable, still stunned by the poisoned knowledge I learned as a child about the preternatural obsessiveness of Jew-hatred, about humanity's capacity for self-annihilation.

And yet I am more profoundly astonished by the capacity of the survivors—as individuals, as a people—to crawl out of the abyss and rebuild. And not just rebuild but transcend: the creation of Israel, the greatest Jewish dream, immediately following the greatest Jewish nightmare. I believe that in the future, Jews will celebrate our return home the way we celebrate today the ancient Exodus from Egypt, except perhaps with greater awe.

And so, neighbor, our annual Holocaust commemoration isn't about clinging to victimhood but the opposite: reaffirming the Israeli commitment to never again be victims. That is at the heart of the Israeli ethos.

The founders of Zionism didn't blame anti-Semites for the Jewish condition; they faulted the Jews. Without sentimentality, the early Zionists looked at the flaws in the Jewish character, developed over centuries of homelessness and insecurity, and set out to transform their people. Jews were resented as economic middlemen? Get them to work the land. Jews were physically threatened? Teach them to protect themselves. It doesn't matter what the gentiles say, Ben-Gurion admonished, but what the Jews do.

The most beloved Zionist poet, Hayim Nahman Bialik, came to prominence as a young man with a poem he wrote in 1903, "In the City of Slaughter," a howl of rage about a pogrom that same year in czarist Russia. Bialik's anger was directed not against the murderers but the victims, whom he faulted for passivity. It is hard to imagine a national poet writing more bitter words to his people than the young Bialik's taunt: "To the graveyard, beggars! And dig up the bones of your fathers / and the bones of your holy brothers and fill your sacks / and bear them on your shoulders and set forth / and display them in all the fairs . . . / and beg for the pity of the nations and pray for the mercy of the gentiles."

This abhorrence for victimhood is one of the key reasons for Israel's existence, and for its ongoing success. In the face of relentless and sometimes overwhelming threat, Israelis maintain the pretense of daily life. One morning recently there was a terrorist stabbing at the light rail station near my home. About an hour later I went to the station, expecting to see police, ambulances, agitated crowds. Nothing: The blood had been wiped off the pavement, and people were waiting for the next train.

I live among heroes who don't consider themselves heroes at all. My neighbor, Aliza, came here as a girl from Kurdistan, just before the creation of the state; her mother, a widow, decided to raise the children in Jerusalem, where they arrived after weeks of travel by donkey through Iraq and Syria and Lebanon, hungry and ragged but home. Or my friend Shula, who was twelve years old when her family began walking from their Ethiopian village toward Zion, and who for weeks carried her little brother on her back. Or my friend Alex, who sat in the Gulag for organizing classes in Hebrew, an illegal language in the Soviet Union. As a former American Jew, I am among the most privileged of Israelis, scarred mostly by inherited memories. I came to Israel to be among those who refused to be defeated by history.

For me, the embodiment of the Israeli character is a young man I knew many years ago named Hemi, the father of a friend of my daughter's in elementary school. Hemi had been shot in the spinal cord in an army training accident. He married his nurse and, in his wheelchair, became an extreme sportsman. And then he helped found an organization to encourage handicapped Israelis to adopt extreme sports, too.

Not that we don't pay a high price for living under extremity. The Israeli character can be edgy, aggressive; my wife, Sarah, who grew up in genteel Connecticut, calls Israel the post-traumatic stress capital of the world. We cut each other off on the road and in lines. Our politics can be brutal, each side denouncing the other as enemies of Israel. There is growing violence in our schools. Political corruption is on the rise. We live with accumulated layers of unresolved trauma—wave after wave of immigrants entering a country facing the constant threat of terrorism and missile attacks and, every few years, outright war.

A less resilient society would almost certainly have cracked under the strain. But a people that can emerge from its own grave more vitalized than at almost any time in its history—that is a people that can deal with anything.

There is a dark side to Holocaust memory, which President Rivlin was warning against, and I know it well. It is fear—that the Jewish people will once again find itself as alone in the world as we were in the 1940s, when the only ones who seemed interested in the fate of the Jews were their murderers; that we can never escape being the permanent Other.

I have tried over the years to free myself from

those Holocaust nightmares. I have gone so far as to stop watching Holocaust films and reading Holocaust memoirs. (Sarah says I'm like an addict who needs to avoid temptation.) I keep reminding myself: It's over.

But the fears keep returning. And what incites those fears most of all is the war against Israel's existence and legitimacy.

Two elements were essential in preparing the way for the Holocaust. The first was the criminalization of Jewish existence. Though the Nazis plundered the Jews—even corpses were stripped of their hair and gold teeth—the war against the Jews wasn't primarily intended for any tangible gain. The goal of the Holocaust was the Holocaust itself. Toward the end of the war, as Germany was about to lose, the Nazis diverted men and trains from the front to hasten the transport of Jews to the death camps, worried that some Jews might survive. In acting with such single-minded purpose, even against their own self-interest, the Nazis were motivated by an almost messianic sense of mission to free humanity of its greatest threat, the Jews. If the crime was existence, then the only possible punishment was death.

The second element that made the Holocaust possible is the peculiarity of anti-Semitism, which isn't mere hatred of Jews but their transformation into symbol—for whatever a given civilization considers the most loathsome human qualities. And so for precontemporary Christianity, The Jew was Christ-killer. For Soviet Communism, The Jew was capitalist. For Nazism, The Jew was race polluter.

That pattern has played itself out in our conflict. Criticism of Israeli policies, of course, isn't anti-Semitic, and I know of no serious Israeli who thinks it is. (We can be our own most vociferous critics.) But denying Israel's right to exist, turning the Jewish state into the world's criminal, and trying to isolate it from the community of nations—that fits the classic anti-Semitic pattern. When Palestinian leaders call the creation of Israel one of the great crimes in history and refer to the "seventy-year occupation" that began with its birth; when pro-Palestinian demonstrators around the world chant, "From the river to the sea, Palestine will be free," with the clear message that there is no place for a Jewish state—then the terms of the conflict aren't about policies but existence. Israel isn't just accused of committing crimes; it is a crime. From there the next step is inevitable: In the era of human rights, when the international community sees racism as the worst of all sins, the Jewish state becomes the symbol of racism, arch-violator of human rights. When the UN routinely votes to criticize Israel more than all other countries combined, it reinforces the notion of the Jewish state as uniquely evil.

In different ways, neighbor, the results for both of us are devastating. The war against Israel's existence has reawakened old demons in new form. When the worst Jewish fears are incited, your suffering becomes, for us, not a tragedy to redress but a threat to rebuff. Rather than get Israelis to face the consequences of occupation, the opposite occurs. Pushed into a corner, we don't respond with flexibility or contrition; we move into survival mode. The war against Israel's legitimacy reinforces our obtuseness. If the anti-Israel criticism is so shrill, then we absolve ourselves of the need to take any criticism seriously. For a people that prides itself on its millennia-old ethical code, that believes in penitence and self-examination, this is a spiritual crisis.

There is good reason for me to be in survival mode. When I look around my borders I see Hezbollah in the north, Hamas in the south, Islamic Revolutionary Guards from Iran on the Golan Heights—all passionately committed to my destruction. Iranian leaders promise that Israel will cease to exist in a matter of decades; on Iranian missiles is painted the slogan DEATH TO ISRAEL. Iran's protégé, Hezbollah leader Hassan Nasrallah, sarcastically invited Jews around the world to move to Israel because it will be easier to kill them all once they are concentrated in one place. One lesson Jews learned from the Holocaust is this: When your enemy says he intends to destroy you, believe him.

And so I have a split screen in my head: On one side there's Israel versus the Palestinians, and I am Goliath and you are David; on the other side of the screen there's Israel versus the Arab and Muslim worlds, and I am David.

Maybe, in different ways, Israelis and Palestinians need to free each other.

In spring 2004, as the second intifada was ending, I participated in a joint pilgrimage to Auschwitz in a group comprising Arab Israelis—Palestinian citizens of Israel—and Jewish Israelis. The initiative came from the Arab side: a Melkite priest from Nazareth, Abuna Emile Shoufani, together with a group of leading Muslim and Christian figures from the Palestinian Israeli community, who were seeking some way to break the growing estrangement between Arabs and Jews within Israel.

I was skeptical: My traumas as an Israeli, I argued, were rooted in the Middle East, not Europe—in exploding buses, not Auschwitz. Still, if Palestinians were willing to take the emotional risk of opening themselves to Jewish trauma, I felt obliged to respond.

Close to three hundred Arabs and Jews set out together. Had there ever been a stranger pilgrimage to Auschwitz? On the bus to the site an Arab woman took the mike: "I've come," she said, "because I fear the anger that is distorting me." Maybe that's why I came, too: not to save the Middle East but myself.

The tensions were unavoidable: Palestinians were wary of the Holocaust overwhelming their tragedy, Jews were wary of comparisons between the Nakba and Auschwitz, of admitting Palestinians into our deepest trauma. One Arab participant confessed that a friend had warned her, "You'll lose your victim status by going to Auschwitz." A Jewish participant confessed that a friend had warned him, "You're giving away our history by going to Auschwitz with Arabs."

But when we stood together before the crematoria, we hugged and wept. Ali, head of the Arab Scouts movement, took my arm: "Does it make it easier or harder to deal with the past by coming here?" he asked tenderly. Elderly survivors and young Arab men walked hand in hand. We were pilgrims to brokenness, a hope of shared humanity in the place beyond hope.

This was Abuna Shoufani's vision: that the very irrationality of our journey, the suspension of fully justified mutual suspicion, would create a space for

God to work—which is, after all, how miracles can happen. We all called him "Abuna," father—Muslims and Jews, too: On this journey, he was our spiritual father. A Christian with an open heart to both sides had managed to bring Muslims and Jews together in Auschwitz.

The result of our risk taking was an exchange of sensibilities. Jews acknowledged that Auschwitz isn't just a Jewish but a universal wound, while our Arab partners discovered in themselves Jewish rage. Where was the world? they demanded.

We spoke together in Hebrew; however uneasily, we were, after all, fellow Israelis. One older Arab woman, addressing the Jews in the group, said: "From the moment I first met Jews I loved you; but you didn't seem to want me to love you." It was a painful moment of realization: This is how Jewish insularity can be experienced by outsiders.

One of Abuna's implicit intentions was to challenge the "Holocaust denial" widespread in Palestinian society and throughout the Muslim world. I regard Holocaust denial as a backhanded affirmation of the Holocaust's uniqueness, its literal unbelievability. In the West, Holocaust denial is the currency of crackpots; in the Muslim world, from Egypt to Iran, its message is broadcast on state television. The attitude toward the Holocaust in parts of the Muslim world could be summed up, only half-ironically, this way: It never happened, we're glad it did, and we're going to do it again.

Just how deeply the poison has penetrated was evident even in our own group. During one of our nightly processing sessions, an Arab participant said: "I always assumed the Jews were exaggerating about the Holocaust. I thought, it was a tragedy, but innocent people always die in war. But now . . ."

Our Palestinian partners in the pilgrimage to Auschwitz were telling us: We are not at war with Jewish existence. We will not side, even indirectly, with those who tried to erase you from history. We are ready to hear your story, to live together as neighbors. But we need you to see us, too; we need you to hear our story and our pain. Without resorting to foolish and unnecessary historical comparisons. Each side in its wound.

Abuna was trying to help us see in each other the face of suffering humanity. He was offering us a way to free each other.

In the end, did it matter that Arabs and Jews went to Auschwitz? Aside from the participants, who even remembers?

Abuna taught me to believe that any spiritual initiative, done with purity of intention, can have unintended consequences. Muslims and Jews—in the midst of an intifada—actually did this together. That gesture of radical goodwill, that defiance of political common sense, is now part of the story of Arabs and Jews in this land. And by writing to you now, I am passing on that memory of the possible.

# A Booth at the Edge of the Desert

Dear Neighbor,

It is the holiday of Sukkot, the festival of booths, when Jews build temporary shacks as extensions of our homes. The holiday recalls the journey of the Israelites through the desert on their way to this land, and shacks evoke the structures that sheltered them in their wanderings. For a full week, the sukkah becomes a surrogate home, in which we eat and host friends and study Torah and sometimes even sleep.

My family builds its sukkah on our porch facing your hill. Perhaps you can see the fragile structure from your home: poles holding up a roof of palm branches laid on wooden slats, with walls of printed cloth.

The side of our sukkah facing your hill is left entirely open. And so throughout the week I live with a heightened sense of intimacy between our hills. In the morning, I hear the cries of Palestinian children playing in the schoolyard. I can clearly see into the new apartment buildings that rise above the wall, built to defy constriction but mostly standing empty. The call to prayer seems to be coming from within the sukkah. The desert just beyond your hill extends like our shared backyard.

The sukkah is a reminder of fragility, transience. And yet leaving the comfort of one's home for the holiday also implies a trust in the benign nature of the world, in Divine protection. And so in the Jewish imagination the sukkah is a symbol for a redeemed world, where human beings will have learned to live with each other in peace. Spread Your sukkah of peace on us, we pray.

Every family decorates its sukkah in a distinctive way, reflecting its understanding of Jewish identity and aspirations. Sukkahs of the ultra-Orthodox tend to have photographs or drawings of prominent rabbis; others decorate their sukkahs with symbols of harvest.

Our family's sukkah reflects the theme of human oneness. In the ancient Temple, priests on Sukkot would offer sacrifices for the well-being of the nations. And so Sarah and I bring some of the world's sacred traditions into our temporary home. Hanging from its wooden roof is an arc of Tibetan prayer flags, which our daughter, Moriah, brought home from the Himalayas—along with Tibetan flags imprinted with a Hebrew prayer for the well-being of humanity. A decorated elephant, Hindu symbol of the primal energy of creation, dangles from a thread, beside a shofar, or ram's horn, a Jewish call to spiritual awakening. And on the wall connecting my study with the sukkah hangs a ceramic plaque with one of the most beloved verses of the Qur'an: "His eternal power extends over the heavens and the earth, and their upholding wearies Him not." All reinforce the same message of a world in harmony with itself and its Creator.

And yet, sitting in my sukkah, I sometimes feel more exposed than protected. From my porch, I clearly see three distinct political entities. The sovereign territory of the state of Israel ends at the wall. In the distance is the Palestinian Authority. And in the farthest distance, the hills of Jordan.

Just beyond my field of vision is a Middle East in ruins. Syria is a graveyard, Iraq is devouring itself, a mad dictator in Turkey is destroying his country's elite, Yemen is starving. . . . What future, neighbor, can our two peoples create here?

It is a bright, cool October morning. Clouds are forming, a relief after six months without rain. I sit on a pillow on the floor of the sukkah, surrounded by Sarah's plants—thyme and hyssop, pomegranate and olive saplings. In one hand I hold a palm branch, flanked with willow and myrtle branches; in the other, a citron, whose sweet and pungent scent seems to fill the sukkah. The Bible instructs Jews to assemble these "four species" for this harvest season. In our prayers, we wave them in the four directions and then toward Heaven and earth, blessing the land and its inhabitants.

The rabbis offer symbolic interpretations of each of the four species—the citron, for example, is said to represent the heart; the palm, the spine. And yet those explanations, however poetic, are somehow beside the point. What matters to me at this moment is that these are the fruits of the land through which Jews for millennia have sought to transmit blessing. The ritual feels even older than the Bible, a remnant perhaps of a shamanistic tradition. I cherish the way it transforms me into someone archaic, a contemporary of the past. It's the same experience I enter every Friday night, when I withdraw from secular time into Shabbat, suspending the use of computer and cell phone and car, becoming temporarily premodern.

Head covered in prayer shawl, I point the palm frond slowly, in a clockwise direction, encompassing the Middle East. I pray for the shattered peoples around me, but most of all I pray for us, for your people and mine. *Ana Adonai hoshiya na*: Please, God, save us.

The world is burning, neighbor. Not only our tortured corner of the planet; everywhere, despair is rising. Our generation possesses a terrible knowledge: We know that humanity can destroy itself. Nuclear war? Environmental devastation? It seems that we are only gradually absorbing the terrifying difference between this and all other times that preceded us. Perhaps we'd be incapable of going through our daily routines if we fully acknowledged the nature of the threat, just as we need some filter to avoid a constant brooding over our own mortality.

And yet this is also a time when one can imagine humanity transcending itself. With our scientific and technological achievements, we can conceive of an end to hunger and disease. The world is in instant communication with most parts of itself, a kind of telepathy. When natural disaster hits one country, others immediately respond—an entirely new reality.

When the children of Israel entered this land, Joshua divided the twelve tribes into two groups. Six tribes ascended Mount Gerizim, the "mountain of blessing," and six ascended Mount Ebal, the "mountain of curse." In the valley below, priests proclaimed the moral imperatives of the Torah. Turning toward the tribes on

Mount Gerizim, the priests declared: "Fulfillment of these laws will bring blessing." The people responded, "Amen." Turning toward the tribes on Mount Ebal, the priests declared: "Violation of these laws will bring curse." And once again the people said, "Amen."

The ceremony marked the moment that a people meant to be consecrated entered a land intended to be holy. And the message was: Choose blessing. Choose life.

It seems to me, neighbor, that all of humanity is now standing on those two mountains.

The desperate nature of our postmodern time intensifies my feeling of responsibility as a carrier of an ancient story. What does it mean for humanity that the Jews have maintained a core identity and consistent memory over four thousand years? What wisdom does my people, history's ultimate survivors, need to offer now?

Since biblical times, Jews have believed we were intended to be a blessing to humanity. What does that sense of self require of us in our relationship with you? What initiatives must I take to try to bring us closer to peace once again, despite all the odds? That is the challenge of Sukkot to me as a Jew living in Jerusalem.

The very act of building and inhabiting the sukkah is an expression of defiance against despair. This open and vulnerable structure is the antithesis of the fortified concrete room in my basement, which every Israeli family is required by law to build, against possible missile attacks. We live with that threat as a constant reality. But the sukkah is our spiritual air raid shelter, promise of a world without fear.

In these letters, neighbor, I have tried to convey to you something of why being Jewish and Israeli is so important to me, why I draw so much strength from the intensity of those commitments.

And yet I try to remind myself that, in the end, along with our personalities and achievements, the soul will leave all our mortal identities behind. So long as we walk this earth, we honor those identities and loyalties. But being a religious person also requires maintaining some relationship with our souls, to the core of our being that is indifferent to all the identities we cherish. Can we draw on our souls, neighbor, to help us overcome our wounds and our fears? What is our responsibility as religious people in a land sanctified by the love and devotion and expectations of myriads of souls through the centuries? What is our responsibility as "custodians" of one of humanity's most intractable conflicts, in the most dangerous moment in history?

It is just past 4:00 a.m. Another night without sleep. My nightmares come to me when I lie awake.

And here, suddenly, is the muezzin, like an old friend, filling the space between our hills with the predawn prayer. I want to thank him for the gift of his call, accompanying me through restless nights.

And so, dear neighbor, I end these letters as I began: with the prayer that we will meet. Now we have spent some time together in spirit, but I hope to host you one day in my home—in my sukkah. *B'ezrat Hashem.* With God's help. *Inshallah.*

# Letters from Palestinians to Their Israeli Neighbor

Dear Reader,

The following is a selection from the written responses
I've received to this book from Palestinians and others
around the Middle East. Those letters express, in turn,
deep anger, goodwill, and passionate but respectful
disagreement. One young woman from Gaza posted
on my Facebook page, "I'm reading your book because
I hope it will give me hope."

Inevitably I received my share of hate messages: Jews
have no history in this land, the army of Mohammed is
returning to slaughter you. Those curt messages sound
more or less the same. Far more interesting are the long
emails I've been receiving from Palestinians. Those

letter writers are obviously a self-selecting group—
willing to engage not only with an Israeli but, however
critically, also with the Zionist narrative. I have no idea
how widespread their attitudes are among Palestinians
and am wary of drawing far-reaching conclusions. For
me, the significance of these letters is simply this: I set
out to find partners with whom I could model a respectful argument over competing narratives. Those partners
exist.

These letters are not easy for me as an Israeli to
read. But each response has given me another insight
into the complexity of our situation.

Given the profound bitterness of this conflict, I
have resolved to treat any response that isn't hateful
as an opening, however slender, to conversation. My
wife, Sarah, calls this book a letter in a bottle tossed
over the wall. I initially wrote to an anonymous Palestinian, with the hope that, through this book, our
mutual anonymity would end. That process has begun, and I now know the names and faces and stories
of some of my neighbors.

Some Palestinian respondents requested anonymity, concerned that any engagement with Israelis—
even critical engagement—might compromise their
place in their society. That, too, is part of this story.

In addition to letters, three groups of young Palestinians, from Jerusalem and the West Bank, have formed study circles to read and discuss this book. Together with friends, I am working on intensifying those efforts.

The letters that follow were written mostly by Palestinians, though I've included several letters from others in the region. I've responded to each letter writer, and in some cases, an ongoing correspondence has resulted. In those exchanges I have argued the narrative that is the basis of this book, and debated aspects of the Palestinian narrative as expressed in the following letters. But I haven't included my responses here. Instead, it seemed right to honor the generous spirit of these letter writers by ending the book with their words.

And so *Letters* has evolved into its next stage: a document of two narratives. My hope is that this book will offer a new language for Palestinians and Israelis to navigate their competing and perhaps irreconcilable narratives—not through zero-sum debate, where each side tries to expose the flaws of the other, but through discussion and listening. Not to convince the other but to allow each side to understand how the other understands and experiences the conflict.

I am deeply grateful to those Palestinians who responded to this book's invitation to model a respectful conversation about our profound disagreements. I look forward to continuing this hard and necessary experiment together.

—Y.K.H.

Dear Future Neighbor,

I call you "future neighbor" because we aren't yet neighbors. Neighbors live in equality. Neighbors have shared rights and duties. Neighbors share moments of joy and check on each other in times of distress.

As long as Israel continues to occupy me and my people, we can't be neighbors. But I want to be your neighbor, and I hope that one day we will be. And so I write to you now, my future neighbor.

Let me tell you something about myself. I am a Muslim, Arab, Palestinian raised in a refugee camp. But my family is rich when it comes to care and compassion. I grew up in the beautiful land of Palestine. I grew up loving my identity, my history, and my culture. I can still hear the echo of my grandfather's stories about the glory of the olive trees in his home, which he had to flee in 1948. My grandfather planted a seed of love for my country that has grown to be a strong tree in my heart.

When my grandfather became a refugee, he was a

newly married man. He left with his pregnant wife, my grandma, who gave birth to her firstborn child in a cave outside Bethlehem. Yes, like Jesus. My grandfather constantly reminded me of his home that he left, the village he grew up in, the key that he closed his house with when he left for the last time.

Growing up I often asked myself, What does my grandfather want me to do with his key? Does he want me to fight for it? He had a moral claim that the UN General Assembly recognized in Resolution 194. Do I need to die for this claim? What is my moral responsibility and the action I need to take to honor my story?

On the one hand, I can't reject my grandfather's story. It is my heritage. I measure my life against the values I learned from my family, our experience as refugees. But I also have a moral responsibility toward building a better future. What do I do with "the right of return"? I could say that my family's claim is the only legitimate story in this conflict. That no one else has a claim except me and I must fight against any other claim, to be ready to kill and to die for my exclusive claim to justice.

I'm young enough to dream and believe that peace is possible and fear can be overcome. I'm also old enough to have my own terrible experiences from living in a refugee camp under occupation.

For my grandfather, the right of return to what is now the state of Israel was the only solution to the Palestinian refugee problem. For me, the issue is more complicated. I need to honor my grandfather's story, but still have ownership over my future. I must separate his past, my past, from the future. Separate the "right" from the "return."

I want the whole world, including Israelis, to honor my grandfather's story and his legitimate claim to all of the historical land of Palestine. At the same time, we Palestinians need to compromise on the return to create space for two countries. For us to be neighbors.

There are only two options. Live in the past and die fighting for your claim or live for a hopeful future building my state next to yours.

Just as I expect you to hear my story, I need to be ready to hear yours. The Palestinian story is precious, but so is the Jewish story. As you write in your book, you too believe the whole land belongs to your people. Our conflicting claims to the same piece of land leave us no choice but compromise.

For a long time, I resisted accepting that the Jews were a real people. I asked myself, How can Jews after four thousand years of being different colors, from different backgrounds, speaking different languages, still insist on the idea of peoplehood? It didn't make sense to me. My experience under occupation, with checkpoints and settlements and a daily dose of fear, never allowed me to give serious thought to your people and your story.

Growing up I was constantly reminded by my own media, educational system, even the graffiti on the walls of the refugee camp, that the Jewish peoplehood idea is the ultimate contradiction to my story. That accepting any part of your story is not compromise but denial and destruction of my story.

But in the last years I decided to use the key my grandfather left me to unlock a peaceful end to our conflict. I decided to stop pointing my finger and try to genuinely understand your story. I met Israelis and built meaningful relationships with Jewish friends. After attending Jewish holiday and Shabbat dinners, it became clear to me that Jewish peoplehood is the cornerstone of Jewish traditions, culture, collective memory and identity. Denying Jews their right to define themselves as a people is not a political tactic; it is an attack on the heart of Jewish identity.

Your letters are genuine and honest. Thank you for opening yourself to your readers and inviting a response from your future Palestinian neighbors. I never thought I would be writing this to you, but your friendship and genuine interest in my story made me overcome my fears and more honestly share my own thoughts.

Palestinian acceptance of Jewish peoplehood is not something to be demanded or gained through the political process. Rather, it is something which can best be secured through friendship and connection.

Every time the Israeli prime minister demands recognition of the Jewish state without any mutual recognition of our own Palestinian national identity as people he only increases the gap between us. Only genuine voices like yours will help Palestinians recognize the Jews as a people.

We both have legitimate claims. I understand that for Jews the West Bank and Gaza are part of the land of Israel, while for my people, pre-1948 Palestine is engraved with our culture, history and stories.

The single-story approach, which leaves room for only one narrative, for only one truth, is very dangerous. As you write, this conflict is between right and right. The whole world, including the Palestinians, should recognize the Jews' religious, political and peoplehood identity and claim to the land of Israel. But the Jewish people have to differentiate between the land of Israel and the state of Israel. Both sides must open the space for tough, honest discussion.

Thank you for writing a book that helps us have that discussion.

Signed,

Your future neighbor

*The author, who has been active in efforts to boost the Palestinian economy, requests anonymity.*

Dear Yossi,

Thank you so much for the book and for the kind handwritten note. I have read the book three times. Once with my Palestinian hat on, once with my attempting empathy hat on, and just now as a rookie book critic, and I find my reaction to it full of duality too.

There is a deep agreement with much of it. Of course Israelis must tell their own stories: I insist on this myself when Israelis tell me that I am Lebanese, not "fakestinian"—"How about I tell you who I am and you ask why that is?" Israel is as legitimate as any other country. (But in its present form it inflicts brutality and apartheid on another country and there is the confusion with its legitimacy. Was apartheid South Africa legitimate? Is Tibet legitimately part of China?

Right now, until it makes peace and redefines its borders it is only legitimate inside the '67 borders and most importantly only in West Jerusalem.) Sharing our stories, but even more crucially, listening with empathy to each other's stories, is sorely needed. I couldn't believe more in those things. Equally, I couldn't believe more in opposing Israel and isolating it as much as I can. Far, far, faaaar more than anything—I want the pain to end. But my view is that Israel, in its current apartheid form, will never withdraw and stop dishing out the pain.

I lingered over the meanings of and emotions connected to the Jewish holidays you described in your book, and I savored the sadness, the pride and the determination. I mourned for your losses and celebrated your wholeness. I enjoyed your personal stories, the writing styles that you use, and at least you touched upon some of the less desirable aspects of your society. My heart ached over the description of the trip to Auschwitz and the deep human connections that are possible between two peoples that have suffered so much. The heart is infinitely more powerful than the mind if only we would allow it to be so.

But it is also true that I felt strong disagreement with some of what you wrote. Just as you say Israelis seethe at Mahmoud Abbas's perceived omissions, misinterpretations and distortions, I too seethed sometimes. I see your position on the '67 war not as omissions and misinterpretations but as outright disingenuity (sorry). I find it very hard to believe a person such as yourself doesn't know the truth of the '67 war. I quoted enough Israeli generals and politicians in my last letter to you, so I won't quote too many this time.

Here is a sample:

Mordechai Bentov: "The entire story of the danger of extermination was invented in every detail, and exaggerated a posteriori to justify the annexation of new Arab territory."

General Matti Peled: "To claim that the Egyptian troops massed at the border could in any way threaten the existence of Israel is not only an insult to the intelligence of any person capable of analyzing this type of situation, but above all an insult to the Israeli army."

General Mordechai Hod: "For sixteen years, we had been planning what took place in those first 80 minutes. We lived with that plan, we ate with it, we slept with it. We never stopped improving it."

Was it only Israeli children who were tortured beyond recognition? Were peace offers only ever offered by one side? Would it be remotely possible for leaders to agree (or have the mandate) to give half of their country to others and can you blame them for refusing?

Is it true that only one side wanted peace? Is it true that Israel didn't/doesn't want war with its neighbors? Can it be true that Palestinians are so insane? And on and on . . . Can you possibly see history like that, or are you being even more disingenuous than Mr. Abbas? You will have to correct me (again, I hope) but my logical head says there is more than a little propaganda (well disguised I suppose), fashioned delicately and lovingly, and woven skillfully into a vest that says, "It is all their fault so they deserve all the brutality they get from us." Yossi, I suppose slipping some propaganda into your book was too tempting an urge to ignore, or was it your intention all along?

I am sure that you have received much praise for your book (and deservedly so), and certainly I am no wordsmith or historian, but here are a few things that perhaps may not be too obvious to mention:

I would never presume to tell a Jew how they should feel about Israel but I have asked more than a few. I get that my Jewish friends, who are active with me in the movement to boycott Israel, are atypical and perhaps viewed as a dangerous fringe (and maybe traitors?). But they do exist in growing numbers and they insist on being counted as Jews and being heard. They experience their Jewishness as belonging to a global family, as you have described, but they feel English or Australia first, Jewish second and Israeli not at all. I asked them if they agreed that Israel was "the home of the Jewish people." Most of them said to me that Israel was just the home of some Jewish people, they never had any intention of moving there and many of them had never even visited. I'm sure you can point to polls which show that the majority (probably in decline) do view Israel as their spiritual home, but perhaps we can agree that there is a significant minority that don't. My understanding of the home of THE Jewish people is that it is Earth. The sooner all peoples view the Earth as their home first and foremost, and that all people belong to the same tribe, the sooner we will have some peace and understanding. Is that view so utopian that it is just unattainable? Perhaps, but I was always told to dream big and so I do not raise my daughter to be half Palestinian; I am raising her to be fully of the tribe of the Earth. Perhaps we are in a race to achieve this before we destroy the Earth?

Yossi, of course I believe in the two-state solution. Yes, I agree that Palestinians shouldn't return to Israel, but I think there should be compensation, peacekeepers, East Jerusalem as our capital, agreed land swaps, and access to the mosque. But MOST importantly, it needs to happen now. No road maps, no time frames, just happen now. Right now. Anything that delays it from happening right now is just facilitating the brutality of my people. The starting point is ceasing settlement building, withdraw from all areas where your people do not live and leave our areas to the peacekeepers; then we can negotiate land swaps. But I will not spend my time promoting anything that doesn't include immediate withdrawal of occupation forces. That's all I will support; the rest is a media game that Israel plays while it takes everything it wants. But yes, a two-state solution with land swaps and Israel keeping most of its occupiers in place—but not all.

We both know that Israel wants to make a few Gazas out of Palestine and call it peace. That's not going to work for you or for me. The one-state solution is only grudgingly supported by those who believe that Palestine is now impossible because of Israel's settler invasion and Israeli ultra-nationalism and racism, and perhaps by our utopian brothers and sisters. Why do you think people who boycott don't want viable a two-state solution?

In my experience, it is Jews who do not believe in a two-state solution. I have never met any Palestinian who has said that we should fight Israel for Tel Aviv or Haifa. What an insane proposition that is! Saying something is illegitimate doesn't mean denying yourself the possibility of ever being free and instead, inflicting pain and death without hope on your children forever. How many Israelis think Palestine is legitimate? Yossi, please do the hypocrisy test with me on this one. Every way that you can point the finger at us legitimacy-wise (as with most things?), Israel is the main perpetrator. How many Israelis believe in a fair two-state solution? How many Israelis believe in the legitimacy of Palestine? How many Israelis would even *say* the word "Palestine"? Actually, how many Israelis think we are inferior and we don't even *deserve* freedom? Israel lacks THE most basic starting position of people who want to make peace. I firmly believe that if you and I were to somehow smash out a fair solution and were able to put it to our people, the overwhelming majority of Palestinians would say yes but the majority of Israelis would give a resounding no. Please do stop talking about legitimacy unless you are saying how the world shouldn't trust Israel to make peace because they vehemently deny the legitimacy of Palestine. This conversation really is nonsense to me until I hear the word "Palestine" uttered by the Israeli government. We have recognized you; you refuse to even say our name. Catch up with us; we are leading the way with legitimacy.

All the best, Yossi, and the best of luck in your future endeavors. I hope to be reading more of your lovely writing and I really do send you some genuine brotherly love and heartfelt human validation.

With respect and friendship,

Subhi

*Subhi Awad grew up in a Palestinian refugee camp in Beirut and lives in Byron Bay, Australia, where he works as an accountant and is an activist in the movement to boycott Israel.*

Dear Yossi,

You wrote that "one of the main obstacles to peace is an inability to hear the other side's story." I agree with you. In my search to understand how this fate befell my own family, I have studied and questioned Palestinian nationalism and its associated narrative, as well as the story of Jewish nationalism and the significance of the Land of Israel in Jewish identity. It is clear that both sides' public narratives—or "conventional wisdom"— have been infected by a century of propaganda, like all nationalist histories are to one degree or another, even in the scholarly sphere.

The lingering impact of one hundred years of "fake news" on both sides has undermined the ability for either side to see the other as we see ourselves, to humanize and empathize, and to begin to trust. This, in my view, is the key ingredient needed before this chapter of history can be closed.

I agree with you that the occupation will only end when the majority of Israelis believe it should, and that that will not happen until Israelis have dispensed with the belief that a Palestinian state will likely be irredentist and itself a potential existential threat to Israel. This requires vigorous opposition to the misinformation on the Israeli side of the historical narrative.

Your letters are replete with historical mistakes and nationalist clichés. You are obviously not, to use your rhetorical straw man, "a pathological liar without any history." You simply come across as choosing to ignore the many nuances and uncertainties in the narrative of Jewish and Israeli nationalist history.

Below are critiques of some quotes from your book, in no particular order. The list is far from exhaustive.

On the 1948 borders, you write: "A withdrawal from the West Bank would reduce the Jewish state to vulnerable borders that had repeatedly tempted Arab states to attack us." The borders you refer to—the 1949 armistice lines—were never attacked in the way you are implying, and the temptation "to attack" you accuse the Arab states of was never reached. The closest situation was the few hours of Egyptian-led Jordanian army retaliation after Israel's 1967 destruction of the Egyptian air force. The "tempted" claim presumably refers to the pre-67 bombastic rhetoric of Syria and Egypt and implies knowledge of the Arab states' state of mind; yet all scholarly research which analyzed the Arab leadership in 1967 concluded with certainty that none of the Arab states intended to attack. (The reasons for their idiotic brinkmanship in the lead-up to the war have been well researched and explained.)

On refugees, you write: "Palestinian refugees are the only refugee community in the world whose homeless status is hereditary." This is not correct; it is a propaganda theme cooked up to discredit their status. Children born in UNHCR camps (i.e., the other 60 million refugees you referred to) are counted as refugees too; there is no rule against inclusion. The correct statement is that Palestinians are the only modern group of refugees still in existence whose right of return has been denied for multiple generations. It results in the same fact pattern but sounds very different.

On the wider context, you write: "Meanwhile, other humanitarian emergencies demand attention." This rhetorical technique was known in Soviet times as "whataboutism." At 51 years, Israel's post-67 military occupation, in all its forms, is the longest in the world, as is the Palestinian refugee crisis. Other situations may be more acute, but this is the world's most chronic.

On colonialism, you write: "A majority of Israelis today are descended from Jews who left one part of the Middle East to resettle in another. Tell them that Zionism is a European colonialist movement and they simply won't understand." In 1947, just prior to Israel's establishment, half of all Jewish-owned land was owned by two funds, the Jewish National Fund and the Palestine Jewish Colonization Association. Israel's largest bank, Bank Leumi, was originally known as the Jewish Colonial Trust. There are many other examples of the use of the terms "colony" or "colonial" by the early Jewish immigrants to Palestine. Taking offense at the word "colonialist" is simply not tenable in light of the historical facts.

On the Gaza withdrawal, you write: "That, after all, is what happened when Israel withdrew from Gaza in 2005, uprooting all its settlements and army bases. Yet thousands of rockets were fired for years afterward into Israeli neighborhoods along the border." This juxtaposition is well-known cheap propaganda. You are implying causation, whereas the reality was much more complex. The Israeli political need to play tough in front of its voters poisoned any hope of positive relations between Gaza and Israel. The Sharon-Olmert governments bear partial responsibility for their involvement in intra-Palestinian politics. And the withdrawal itself was only partial; indirect control remained—the world still considers Gaza to be occupied due to Israeli control of its airspace, maritime waters, land borders, electricity, communications networks, population register, etc. The propaganda in Israel around this situation—i.e., the Israeli government's failure to share the blame—is one of the major obstacles to peace today.

On the notion of a "land without a people," you write: "When the conflict began, this land was largely empty. Even as the presence of both Arab and Jewish communities grew, the land was able to accommodate two nations." Another century-old propaganda theme. This nonsense is deeply insulting to Palestinians. Note that the two provinces which made up Palestine in the late nineteenth century—the period you were referring to—were the 4th and 7th most populated out of all the Ottoman Empire's 36 provinces. Its then population density was greater than that of contemporary Indonesia, Nigeria and Egypt, today three of the most overpopulated countries in the world. And today, excluding the micro-states, Israel and the occupied territories is the fourth most densely populated country in the world, behind only Bangladesh, Taiwan and Lebanon. The above is intended to give an example of how deep and broad the narrative problem is. There is a lot of work to do.

None of these narrative corrections are original—I believe you have heard many of the counterpoints before, and the others have been well known to scholars in their ivory towers for many years. So how and why does such an intellectually advanced society as Israel's allow itself to believe something so impure, filling Jewish children's minds with propaganda and misinformation? It seems that the Israeli mainstream instinctively feel that history is a battle to be won, a negotiation, not an exercise in finding truth or building bridges.

For us as your Palestinian neighbors to respect and accept the Israeli nationalist narrative, it will first have to be diluted. (The same is of course true for the Palestinian narrative.) What I mean by diluted is that those speaking for the Israeli-Jewish community will need to dispense with certainties and binary depictions. As an individual it requires looking deep inside to question narratives which your parents and grandparents believed in until their dying days, and in some cases dedicated their lives to.

The last two decades have shown that Israeli scholars who expose inaccuracies in the Jewish nationalist narrative are ostracized, with their works picked apart to find some unforgivable error with which to beat their research into silence. Whether or not you like them as individuals, trust their motivations, or agree with their overall theses, they have highlighted weaknesses in the Jewish collective memory that must be embraced more widely. By weaknesses, I mean that these scholars have sown reasonable doubt, creating grey areas where people otherwise think and speak in black and white. To talk as neighbors we must move away from certainties and proactively acknowledge these weaknesses in our own narratives. The way your letters are written shows that you have yet to travel far down this path, at least as it relates to the core tenets at the root of Jewish-Israeli identity.

If you want me, as your neighbor, to walk with you on the journey that you suggested, you will need to show evidence of doing the same.

With best regards,

Onceinawhile

*"Onceinawhile" is the pen name of a Palestinian businessman who writes for Wikipedia's "Israel Palestine Collaboration" project, which aims to build consensus around a unified historical narrative.*

Dear Yossi,

It's great that you are calling me neighbor, because in fact we are neighbors even though it took me time to realize it.

I grew up not seeing you as my neighbor. Instead, I grew up in Gaza seeing you as a criminal, as somebody who came to steal our land and kill us. That is what I learned from our history. That's what I have been taught.

And why not believe it?

I was born in 1994 and so was only six years old when the Second Intifada started. I remember being in the UNRWA [United Nations Relief and Works Agency for Palestine] school where every day I was reminded that you kicked my family out of the land.

From the moment the airstrikes started on Gaza, I heard the sounds of bombs, and the screams of my schoolmates. From our school we could see smoke everywhere.

When I returned home from school, I asked my parents to tell me who did this. They told me, "The Jews, the Israelis did it." So why not hate you? Why not see you as an enemy?

Living in Gaza, I had had no human interaction with Israelis. The only Israeli voice I recognized was that of Israeli jets flying overhead.

Now you tell me about the repeated rejections
of the Palestinians to the peace plans offered by the
Israelis—whether by Ehud Barak or Ehud Olmert.

I would like to tell you how Palestinians understand
this in light of our history: We have learned that before
1948 and the establishment of Israel, our "Nakba," or
catastrophe, the whole land of Palestine was ours and
everybody on the land spoke Arabic. Then all of a sud-
den, Palestinians were called upon to approve giving
a large portion of land to foreigners. Can you tell me
why we should have approved such a thing?

It's clear that you and I see the situation completely
differently in terms of how we examine this conflict.
The wall between us doesn't permit those on each side
to see the humanity of the other. Instead, it makes
both sides feel like the other side is his enemy, whom
he should fear.

In my history classes, when I was at school, I
never heard about the Jews having been here or
about them having any connection to the land.
What I have always heard is the word "alhaykal al-
maz'aom," which means the claimed temple, referring to the temple that the Jews claim to have had
in Jerusalem. It wasn't until I became serious, as a
Christian, about reading the Bible that I recognized
that the Jews were here, and they had had the tem-

ple. I actually was angry that our education system would lie to us.

Why do we as Palestinians have to remove a part of the history in order to disprove the connection of the Jews to this land?

It was challenging for me to accept the connection of the Jews to the land and I totally understand the emotional sensitivity of my people who refuse it.

But here is my question: Does the Jewish connection to the land mean justifying complete Jewish sovereignty over the land and outright rejecting Palestinian nationalism? I don't think it should. I think it is wrong to attempt to erase the historical connection of both Jews and Arabs to this land.

Now, I understand your longing for and need of the land as Jews, and personally, I have a lot of sympathy for that. But can you acknowledge the suffering you caused by coming back?

Whether it was the result of war or other systemic actions, once the Nakba happened, 650,000 refugees were not allowed to come back to their homes because you came back to yours.

Can we handle this paradoxical narrative? Can I acknowledge your need and connection to the land, and can you acknowledge the suffering caused to our people because of your return?

I know there are those among the Palestinian people who try to say that Judaism is only a religion. I know there are also those who say that you are not Jews at all.

For me, I reject both of these claims because it is not for me to decide what Judaism is. Instead, you and your history are what you will decide.

It seems to me that a large number of Jews have chosen Zionism as their particular form of nationalism, and I am okay with that.

Also, who am I to tell you that you are not Jews? But let us understand what is at the root of the claims of the Palestinians. To say Judaism is only a religion is to imply that Jews do not need a state. And to say that these Jews are not real Jews is to mean that they have no legitimate connection to the land. Why would Palestinians emphasize these claims? It's that feeling that if we do not, then we will legitimize the very Zionism that has destroyed both our national dream and our right to self-determination. How can we envision an end to the occupation and our capacity of self-determination while admitting these things?

We face many risks to our greatest hopes simply by recognizing Jews as a nation who relate to this land. And that, neighbor, is why your voice is important, because it tells us that being a Zionist doesn't have to mean being against Palestinian rights.

My hope is that your book is a sign that there is a new opportunity for honest and challenging dialogue between our peoples.

Sincerely,

Khalil Sayegh

*Khalil Sayegh was born to a family of Palestinian Christian refugees in the Gaza Strip in 1994, the first year of Palestinian Authority control over the Strip. He currently lives in Ramallah and is a fellow for the Philos Project. This letter initially appeared in The Forward and is reprinted with its permission.*

Dear Yossi,

As the translator of your book into Arabic, I had the rare opportunity, for a Palestinian, to enter into issues of Jewish identity and how Israelis see this conflict. These are issues that we Palestinians often discuss without depth or sympathy—for obvious and understandable reasons, given our situation.

Working on this project taught me a lot about Judaism and Jewish identity. I needed to probe deeply into this topic while reading this book carefully and objectively. I hope that Arab readers do not give up before reaching the end of the book so that they will at least learn something about the other side's history and religion and how those shaped the Jewish character. The way you explained politics and religion by moving between the past, present and future helped me draw some clear understanding regarding the experiences that the Jews had faced throughout history and how those had affected and influenced their identity.

Translating this book has taught me about the Jewish fears that are based on deep traumas. For us, Palestinians, understanding those fears is crucial to creating a just and sustainable solution for our conflict. I say crucial because I witness the negative consequences of these fears and how they affect my day-to-day life and my reality as a resident of the West Bank— consequences that are also crucial for the Israeli side to acknowledge.

I will be lying to you, neighbor, if I hid the difficulties that I faced while translating this book. Becoming your translator required me to focus on delivering your message objectively and to educate about your history and your pain—in my language. If you put yourself in my shoes, I am sure you will understand how emotionally challenging that has been.

For example: Which side should take the initial step toward the other? Should the occupation end first or should we first normalize relations between the two peoples? You support the two-state solution but emotionally consider it unjust to Jewish claims to all of the land; can you understand how, in my eyes, it is also unfair and unjust, both on the emotional and the practical levels? And so: Should we be pragmatic or emotional in seeking an end to this conflict? Which way will cause us less pain and suffering? Since there is no way to measure and compare pain—what pain should be counted in determining the level of justness or injustice of the solution? These questions have caused me endless inner turmoil.

For all my ambivalence, I am proud of being a part of this positive initiative that I hope will bear fruit. I hope this book becomes a platform that allows us, Palestinians and Israelis, to share our pain and our aspirations.

You have delivered your message clearly and successfully—something I envy you for. I think that if we Palestinians could express our pain in such a reasonable and balanced manner, perhaps we could have found a listening ear on your side instead of alienating and pushing you away.

I hope that one day, Inshallah, I will be able to

address you, publicly and without fear, as my "Israeli Jewish neighbor."

Wishing you all the best,

Your neighbor

*The author requests anonymity.*

Dear Neighbor,

When your book of letters reached my door, its pacific tone and language encouraged me to respond, since I found it breaks away from the usual rhetoric Palestinians are accustomed to hearing from their neighbor. You wanted to open a dialogue with an "imagined" Palestinian neighbor living on the other side of the separation wall. In responding to you, my goal is to start a dialogue with a "real" Israeli neighbor living next door, in the spirit of our Holy Qur'an, "And argue with them in a way that is best." (16:125)

You use the word "neighbor" to describe the Palestinians living on the other side of a morbid wall, but are we, in fact, neighbors? You enjoy citizenship of a state, while I am just a Jerusalemite permanent resident in your country, deprived of the rights of citizenship.

I am a Palestinian whose family was forced in 1948

to leave all its possessions behind in West Jerusalem to flee for safe refuge, first in Cairo and then in the Old City of Jerusalem. Luckily, I had a grandfather with an iron will who instead of lamenting the past struggled to rebuild a promising future for himself and his family.

We may disagree on interpreting past events, but we do agree on our objectives for the future. You view the conflict from a Western left-right ideological perspective, and I look at it from a moderate-extremist perspective. Your political perspective separates the Palestinians from the Israelis while my perspective views a tacit alliance between the Palestinian-Israeli extremist conflict camp and the Palestinian-Israeli moderate peace camp.

You argue that the occupation did not create violence but that violence prolonged the occupation. Since the premise is false, the conclusion cannot be valid. The occupation tarnished by subjugation boosted extremism, and extremism espoused hostility and violence.

Have you ever wondered, Yossi, why Palestinians believe they have no other choice to end the occupation except by force? Should you put yourself in their shoes, you would understand why. Palestinians often ask me how do I envision that moderation could end the occupation—a tough question to answer persuasively while confronting on a daily basis expansionist and repressive Israeli policies. Despite the odds, I envisage a culture of moderation would pave the way for reconciliation, which in turn would build trust, leading to negotiations in goodwill, and eventually ushering in peace and prosperity.

You blame the Palestinians for the failure of the Oslo Peace Process, the collapse of the Camp David Summit of 2000, and the 2008 peace plan. This is in line with a quote by former Israeli diplomat Abba Eban, that the Palestinians "never miss an opportunity to miss an opportunity." Allow me to disagree. The blame for missing peace opportunities ought to include Palestinian and Israeli leaders, as well as the Israeli voters and Palestinian masses, who are not psychologically ready for peace nor are they willing to pay the painful price for peace. At the time, when Israeli Prime Minister Olmert offered his peace plan to PA President Mahmoud Abbas in 2008, he lost the elections, obliging both to abandon a viable peace initiative. The maximalist "big dreamers" on both sides again successfully derailed that peace opportunity. From my perspective, "Peace" led by the moderates on both sides confronted "Conflict" driven by the extremists on both sides, and the moderates lost the battle.

I do not share your view that the Second Intifada of 2000 was directed at the existence of the Israeli state. Already in the 1993 Oslo Declaration of Principles, the Palestinians acknowledged the State of Israel, but in its aftermath deep suspicions grew among Palestinians that the right-wing Israeli governments were not serious in implementing the peace agreements signed by its left-wing governments. If you as a moderate held these negative perceptions about Palestinian intentions, then you can imagine how harmful the stereotype image of Palestinians among the Israeli radicals.

As for the persistent claim that Israel withdrew from the Gaza Strip, yet rockets kept being launched from Gaza against Israeli cities and neighborhoods: You have to remember, my friend, that Israel *unilaterally* withdrew from Gaza, handing it on a silver platter to the extremist religious movement Hamas. Hamas propaganda claimed it was the suicide operations rather than diplomacy which forced the Israeli withdrawal. That mantra boosted the image and prestige of Hamas among the Palestinian masses, particularly the youth, in a time of humiliation, despair and poverty.

Each side still does not acknowledge that both Israel and Palestine are the "rightful claimants" to the land for historical and emotional reasons. I share your conviction that Israel has a right to exist and be a country. Contrary to what Palestinians learn and hear, Jews were here in the past and are not newcomers to the land. They have dreamed over many centuries of returning to Jerusalem. They have come here in successive waves of immigration, many from nations that persecuted them.

I hope that you, my neighbor, will also share my conviction that Palestine has a right to exist and be a country. Similar to Jews, Palestinians are not newcomers to the land. Contrary to what Israelis learn and hear, Palestinians were here in the past and deserve to be here in the present and future. The Jewish dream of a homeland is as valid as the Palestinian dream of statehood.

The critical common bond linking us is empathy. The insistence on compassion with the stranger appears with high frequency in the Torah and the Qur'an. I do not share the false claims, often heard in Palestinian society, that "the Holocaust never occurred," or that "the numbers of Holocaust victims are exaggerated," or that it is "the Jews who are to be blamed for the Holocaust because of their function in society, which had to do with usury, banks, and so on." I express my deep empathy with the victims of this calamity. On the other hand, Jews should realize that the 1948 Nakba, without being compared with the Holocaust, left a deep imprint on the psyche of the Palestinians still vivid in their souls. Their persistent traumatic experience as occupied people cannot be matched with their neighbors' traumatic experience during the Holocaust. While Jews view the Holocaust from the "big picture" of seeing it as an evil effort to obliterate them as a people, Palestinians view the Holocaust from the "small picture" of guards, prisons and barbed wire similar to Israeli jails and barbed wire. This necessitates the urgent need for introducing Holocaust education to the Palestinian curriculum.

While your association with Muslim religious scholars reawakened in you the capacity for empathy with your Palestinian Muslim neighbors, it was my journey to Poland, into the abyss of the Holocaust in Auschwitz, that reawakened in me my personal capacity for identification with my Israeli neighbor—a compassion which decades of conflict and strife had suppressed.

Your association with Muslims taught you they generally don't know much about the Jewish culture, identity, and faith and their essential connection to the land. On the other side, my association with Jews taught me what Jews generally know about Islam is to a great extent a misinterpretation of the verses in the Holy Qur'an dealing with Jews. Nearly a decade ago, I participated in a conference on anti-Semitism held at the Hebrew University in Jerusalem. The Israeli expert on Islam who spoke before me argued that the Qur'an was anti-Semitic since it describes Jews as "pigs and apes." When it was my turn to speak, I disputed his claim. He left the conference and later came back holding the Qur'an and interrupted me asking to read the following to prove his point. My explanation was that the verse describes God's punishment for those who transgress the Sabbath only. As it is written: *"And you had already known about those who transgressed among you concerning the Sabbath, and We said to them, 'Be apes, despised.'"* [Qur'an 2:65]

Both neighbors should be willing to make painful concessions and sacrifices to end the conflict and the constant threats of war. One can make peace with another when both mutually agree to acknowledge each other's existence, recognize each other's national concerns and aspirations, and hold a deep respect for each other. Both should hear, learn, and appreciate each other's collective narrative. You study Islam, and I study Judaism. By our journey's end, we will meet in the center and share our love for the religion.

Both would recognize the legitimacy of each other's claims to the land, and neither would seek to obliterate or destroy one another. Both would adopt a peace and reconciliation education curriculum in their schools.

The maps of Palestine would show Israel, and the maps of Israel would show Palestine. Our allegiance would not be to stones or political ideology but would give priority to the human dignity of the other.

For peace between our people to happen and for a shared future to take place, Palestinians, Arabs, and Muslims need to listen to your story and take to heart your letters. Equally important is for the neighbor next door to also acknowledge my identity and rights as well as free access to food, water, shelter, and health care. Both our people need to understand and appreciate the shared connection between the land, the religion, and the identity.

Unfortunately, I doubt that Palestinians will listen to your people's narrative since they are not taught to tolerate the views of people whom they consider their enemies. As you rightly observe, their authorized education, media coverage, religious sermons, and political speeches have constructed a more formidable wall than the cement one your government had built. Palestinian peace activists are the only group prone to understanding "the Jewish story and the significance of Israel in Jewish identity." But they are not your target audience. It will be much more difficult for extremists on both sides to appreciate their "neighbor's" narrative, values, and beliefs.

I share your calls for a new approach to Palestinian-Israeli peacemaking—a strategy that would both respect and limit each people's maximalist claims or what I call "The Big Dream," accommodate the role of religion, and enable each side to listen attentively to the other side's narrative. I am confident that the responses you may receive from close-minded Palestinians and Israelis will not discourage you from continuing your noble efforts to narrow the wide gap between both our people.

We both share the complicated feelings of faith, pride, anger, anguish, and hope. You moved to Israel to participate in the drama of the renewal of a Jewish homeland, and I returned to Palestine to share in making a dream come true. We are both committed to seeing a morally responsible, democratic two-state solution succeed.

The first lesson I learned in grade one of my elementary school was the story of a king taking a walk in the fields coming upon an old man planting an olive tree. He asked him in a teasing manner: "Old man, why are you planting an olive tree? Do you expect to eat any of its fruit?" The old man responded: "Our ancestors planted and we ate, we plant so as our grandchildren would eat." Only recently a rabbi friend of mine drew my attention that the Talmud has similar teaching: "As my ancestors planted for me, so too I plant for my children and my children's children." Let us plant for our children the seeds of peace. Let us join hands to achieve mutual understanding and peaceful relations between our two people based on freedom, justice, and neighborly relations.

With hope and faith,

Your neighbor,

Mohammed S. Dajani Daoudi

*Professor Mohammed S. Dajani Daoudi is founder of the Palestinian peace movement Wasatia.*

*He was the founding director of the American Studies graduate program and general director of libraries at Al-Quds University in Jerusalem. In 2014, he became the center of intense controversy for leading twenty-seven Palestinian students on a visit to Auschwitz. The Palestinian public outcry, accompanied by death threats, led to his resignation from the university.*

Dear Yossi,

I have recently read your book and decided to take up your offer to respond. I am what is sometimes referred to as an "East Bank" Jordanian, meaning that my family does not originate from somewhere in Palestine. I do, however, have many friends and acquaintances who do originally come from there. I grew up most of my life in Jordan. So, in that sense, I may not be your immediate neighbor, but I'm probably the neighbor that is a little down the way from you.

The Palestine/Israel issue has been a fixture of my upbringing for as long as I remember. I cannot think of a time at school where we were not taught about the history of the Arab-Israeli conflict, nor the significant ways it has shaped our current reality. Many of my teachers, after all, were either refugees themselves— and could describe quite vividly their lives as children there—or descendants of refugees and had inherited the stories and history of their exile from Palestine. (Just as you refer to the "land of Israel" in your book as a term that may make your neighbors feel uncomfortable, so, I think, will Palestine be for you.) So, as you can imagine, I got a heavy dose of that history from an exclusively Arab point of view.

Throughout my life, the issue has waxed and waned somewhat, with it waning in my hedonistic years at university in the UK. But the issue has waxed heavily in the last ten years, given my proximity to Palestine/Israel. In an effort to understand the conflict for myself, and in an effort to distance myself from the somewhat simplistic narrative of the conflict given to us during our education, I decided to do some reading of my own. I would start with reading Israeli newspapers, trying to cover the widest possible political spectrum in your country to get a better understanding of how Israeli society thinks. I do feel that I have a basic and general understanding of your people, and your letters certainly helped elucidate the centrality of Israel in the Jewish people's understanding of themselves.

My initial reaction was to send you a reply that would be a point scoring exercise. The comments sections of the internet have convinced me of the futility of such an effort. Instead, I'm just going to say what I feel, in the hope that some of what I say resonates with you.

Let me start with the punch line: I do believe that Israel should exist. That conviction does not come from my basic understanding of the Jewish people or their ties to the land of Israel. It stems, rather, from a basic universal justice I believe in which states that a people with a unique culture deserve to have a unique space where that culture can express itself in a primary manner, where the state reflects the culture of the people it governs. It is also why I have no problem recognizing Israel as the Jewish state. (As an aside, I also believe that the Kurds deserve a state of their own, political and geographical implications for the Arabs, Turks and Iranians be damned.) After all, if the majority of Israel's citizens want to define the state in Jewish terms, who am I to disagree? I would not welcome an Israeli citizen weighing in on how Jordan defines itself, as in fact they sometimes do, when they claim that "Jordan is Palestine."

But . . . and there are a few buts in this letter to you. I do have my reservations and I do disagree with you on the starting point of the reconciliation between Palestinians and Israelis. And that issue concerns, surprise surprise, Zionism. Somewhere in my mind, I can see your eyes rolling and you thinking "Here we go . . . " but hear me out. What I am about to write will most probably be difficult for you to read, and may even offend, but that is not my intent. In your book, you invited Palestinians, Arabs and Muslims to write back to you. I think you should be prepared to hear the other side of the Zionist coin, from our perspective.

To my mind, Zionism is formulated into two parts: the first is the biblical, spiritual yearning for return that formed much of the Jewish experience in exile. The second is the secular need for a *Judenstaat*, as Herzl put it. And each of these formulations has a core problem that, to my mind, has led us to this current situation.

Let me tackle them in order. For the biblical interpretation of Zionism, there is the wish and yearning to return to the land of Israel, for the exile to end and for the Jewish people to be redeemed through the land. I find the fact that Jews have held on to this belief for millennia as laudable, but it is an absolutist and maximalist position. It quite categorically states that "the land of Israel belongs to the people of Israel," which, ipso facto, excludes the people who may be already living on the land that Zionism claims as its own. It is a position that implies that ownership of the land by other people(s), no matter how long, no matter what has been done with the land, no matter their attachment to it, is transient at best and has no historical, practical or legal validity.

Let me now tackle the secular aspect of Zionism, the one that I believe to be far more problematic than the spiritual claims. In a nutshell, secular Zionism dehumanized the Arabs living in Palestine in order to achieve its aims. From the beginning, from the first Zionist Congress in Basel, it was known that there already was another people living on the land—I'm sure you've heard of the infamous phrase "the bride is beautiful, but she is married to another man." Herzl, for his part, viewed the indigenous population of Palestine as a problem to be solved, not as human beings who have the same hopes and fears as the Jews of Europe whom he was trying to protect. To give a quote from Herzl for context: "*We must expropriate gently the private property on the state assigned to us. We shall try to spirit the penniless population across the border by procuring employment for it in the transient countries, while denying it employment in our country. The property owners will come over to our side. Both the process of expropriation and the removal of the poor must be carried discretely and circumspectly . . .*"

What does it say about a national movement, whose professed goal is the salvation and redemption of its people, when it needs to treat the undesirable "*penniless population*" as a mass problem, where their land needs to be "*expropriated*" with secrecy and skulduggery? Of course, other myths and distortions about the Arabs of Palestine grew up around the Zionist dream, most disturbing of all the "land without a people for a people without a land." Did the existence of the people there mean nothing? How could their presence be erased? How dare a people looking for salvation disregard the humanity of another people? Oftentimes, I have heard the reply that the Jews of Europe were facing desperate times, especially with the pogroms in Czarist Russia— but does that truly justify the dehumanization of the people in Palestine? And if the Palestinians in the diaspora were to use the same argument against you—that they are unwanted, unloved, under threat by the various regimes they are forced to live under—would you accept the same formulation of you by them? You do not, in fact. You demand to be seen as human beings, while your national movement has made an entire history around dehumanizing the people you demand see you as human beings.

The undercurrent of these points are two words: Original Sin. Yes, those two words. For me, that is the Original Sin of secular Zionism: that it fails to take into account the humanity of other people in the land it demands for itself. Please understand, I am not asking you to negate or deny Zionism. I cannot ask someone to negate a core principle of their raison d'être and expect to be heard with any seriousness. What I am asking of you is to criticize these aspects of Zionism. No amount of criticism on my part, as an Arab, an outsider, will compel any Israeli or Jew to reflect on the issues that I just raised.

From the Jewish perspective, you never left. You never relinquished your claims to the land, thus temporal and spatial distances are not determinants of who has ownership of the land. Your faith, your belief and your covenant with God are what give you the rights to the land. From the Arab perspective, you are European Jews who came to Palestine from distant shores, and to my mind, that unassailable fact is what gives the

Palestinians the edge in the "justice" wars between the two narratives. The Palestinians did not travel to Europe to claim land that other people were already living on, nor did they have any wish to harm another people, nor spirit the poor ghetto Jews to some other place for their land.

And so, you might think to yourself, how did we get from "I believe the state of Israel should exist" to this point, where this guy is almost negating the spirit of Zionism? Well, ultimately, I do not believe that it would be a just outcome if either the Israelis or the Palestinians won this war. I'm sure you could imagine my objections to the Israelis winning the war, but why the Palestinians? you might ask. Because it won't really solve anything. It won't provide justice to a people that have historically been on the receiving end of injustice; nor will it leave the Palestinians and Arabs with a history to look back on with pride. It will simply leave a gaping wound that we would paper over and ignore the after effects that it would have on us. And who knows, maybe a thousand years from that date, the Jews might return again, and the whole cycle will repeat itself. And so, I come around to the belief that it is better to leave Israel in place than to continue to struggle to remove it.

And so, dear somewhat distant neighbor, how do

we go about resolving our differences, addressing our grievances, and healing our wounds? I'm sorry to say that you are in for some difficult reading up ahead, but it must start with an apology.

No matter how much I slice and dice the issue, analyze it, take it apart and put it back again, my mind again and again returns to this: The Jewish people, those who identify as Zionists at least, must stand up and publicly and sincerely offer a heartfelt apology to the Palestinian people. Regardless of the circumstances you found yourselves in, you took advantage of a poor and relatively powerless people and inflicted a historic injustice against them. A people who, up until the creation of secular Zionism, **had done you no wrong**. There are many things that the Palestinians and Arabs have to apologize to the Jews for, but I do not think that the process can begin without that first step on your part. I sincerely believe that this would be a transformative event between our two peoples. It would finally give the Palestinians the acknowledgment that they have sought and that they surely deserve. Yes, the Arabs should have treated you as returning cousins, brothers and sisters even, but (that damned word again) not without that initial apology can the Arab world begin to concede the wrongs we have inflicted on you.

The last thing I would like to say in this letter is that I am not looking to determine who is more right and wrong on this issue; I am just trying to convey what I think about this complex and bloody conflict, and how I think we can begin to heal. I do believe that in partnership, we could turn the Middle East into the envy of the world, and I do think that ultimately, it is better for the Arabs to reintroduce the spirit of inquiry and self-criticism that you rightly pointed out we have lost. There has been far too much homogeneity in the Arab world over the past century. Injecting something old/new (to paraphrase Herzl) from a people who at their core, I believe, understand us better than any other, will no doubt benefit both our peoples.

Sincerely,

Your Jordanian somewhat distant neighbor

P.S. Why the hell did it take your people so long to reach out to us, the people you will be living in the midst of? Why was this effort not taken at the beginning of secular Zionism, instead of now, when it's almost too late?

*The author, who requests anonymity, is a data analyst living in Amman, Jordan.*

Dear Yossi,

For too long, both sides of this conflict have existed in a kind of self-referencing construct of the imagination. Peace must mitigate the collective distrust between the two peoples, who know little beyond hatred, suspicion, blame and counter blame, fear, paranoia, historical necessity, retribution.

Your willingness to embrace the other stunned me. Every Palestinian needs to read your book. Every Israeli needs to read your book. The Arab world as a whole must read your book. The honesty in your letters, shaped by a powerful sense of redemptive self-searching, is both humbling and inviting.

Still, although I'm Egyptian and cannot presume to speak on behalf of the Palestinian people, I did find certain representational constructs within your narrative which perpetuate convenient myths. I refer you here to the Palestinian writer Raja Shehadeh's thoughtful response to your book in the *New York Times*. He writes, "Your letters seem like an intellectual exercise, which is a privilege that you enjoy but we do not. 'If you were in my place, neighbor, what would you do?' you ask. But we are not in your place. You present the central problem of the conflict as a 'cycle of denial,' in which my side is denying your 'legitimacy,' not sufficiently acknowledging 'Jewish peoplehood,' and yours is denying mine 'national sovereignty.' But those things are not equivalent."

While I agree with Shehadeh's point about the lack of moral equivalency, both sides need to engage in what I call redemptive possibilities. Both sides need to confront, and acknowledge, their own respective contributions to the conflict in order to find a meaningful solution.

Yossi, I believe you have contributed a powerful first step toward redemption. We in the Arab world need to engage in our own collective introspection by acknowledging our shortcomings and failures. This is something we do not do well. I myself engaged in endless arguments against Israel while studying philosophy at Berkeley. I was heavily influenced by Edward Said, particularly his groundbreaking work *Orientalism*.

Over time, however, I grew tired of my own ignorance about the Jewish people. I started reading books about Judaism, Jewish culture, history, and the Holocaust. Something happened along the way—something unpredictable and profoundly transformative. With knowledge came respect, which in turn would lead to an enduring sense of love for the Jewish people. Your own epiphanies and transformative moments, Yossi, are clearly articulated in your book.

In your tenth letter, you write, "Since biblical times,

Jews have believed we were intended to be a blessing to humanity. What does that sense of self require of us in our relationship with you? What initiative must I take to try to bring us closer to peace once again, despite all the odds?" What we need from the Palestinians, as well as the broader Arab world, is that kind of courageous introspection and meditation on the conflict, without the use of accusatory language or recriminations.

Both sides have valid grievances, which must be addressed. But this cannot happen when they are engaged in constant ad hominem attacks. You have stated that your purpose in writing the book was to "explain the Jewish story and the significance of Israel in Jewish identity to Palestinians who are my next-door neighbors." I applaud you for engaging your neighbors who, for too long, have felt marginalized, ignored, and alienated. What we need now are more of these conversations by Palestinians and other Arabs. I am grateful to you for writing such a touching and moving book and for reigniting much-needed optimism in a region where fate seems to have conspired to keep both peoples apart. I believe peace will come, but only if both sides engage in the same kind of redemptive conversation you have started.

Sincerely,

R. F. Georgy

*R. F. Georgy is an Egyptian-American novelist. His lat-est work, Absolution, is being made into a film by the Israeli filmmaker Eran Riklis.*

Dear Yossi,

I have read your book with great interest and with an open heart. As the author of a book about my experiences growing up under occupation in Gaza, I appreciate your attempt to reach out to Palestinians.

The book that I've written is also a kind of letter to the other side. In fact, I end my book with a letter to the Israeli soldier who shot me in the back, without provocation, when I was 15. In my letter I told him that I forgive him and call him "cousin." I hope my book comes out in Hebrew because I want my story known to Israelis. After I was shot, I was treated and rehabilitated in an Israeli hospital, where I experienced the kindness and humanity I didn't know existed on your side.

We have been in contact ever since we spoke to-gether about our books at the United States Institute of Peace in Washington, D.C. We are similar, you and me. We both have a great sense of belonging. I think that this has been the key to your triumph and to my ardent clinging to the idea of Palestine. A Palestine that I believe should exist in peace and dignity side by side with your country.

A few days ago, you wrote to me to check on me and to see how my own book, *The Words of My Father*, is doing. You mentioned that you had just "returned home" from your book tour. I wrote back "Welcome home!" But something paused in me when I wrote that. Your home is not Tel Aviv. You do not even live in West Jerusalem. No, Yossi, you live in East Jerusalem. Your home is land that has belonged to my people for centuries and the world has promised would return to me since it was seized by the Israeli paratroopers whom you wrote about in your previous book, *Like Dreamers*.

We Palestinians are a people of great passion and pride. When you write that the Jews fought an underground war and expelled the British occupiers, you are effectively denying what Palestinians had gone through at the hands of the British colonizers. It is often difficult for me to tell you my story but when I do, I try to tell it to you in terms familiar to you because I truly want you to better understand my narrative.

The more we understand each other's narrative the more of a basis we have to coexist. Our coexistence must not be through denial or separation, but through recognition and integration, and I believe that your book is a profound invitation for such a process. I commend you for that.

It is a wonderful thing to be reminded by you that we both proclaim God's oneness because above all else, that is what's important. I appreciate your connection to God. It brought me closer to your narrative in some profound ways. I invite you to keep on writing letters to the Palestinian people.

The people who fashioned my father's words taught me to love not hate, to never surrender to defeat or injustice, to always stand for peace in the Holy Land, to forgive you for all the pain your people have caused mine and to say to you, "Welcome home, Yossi."

Your Occupied Neighbor,

Yousef Bashir

*Yousef Bashir is the author of* The Words of My Father *(HarperCollins 2019) and a former congressional liaison for the embassy of the Palestine Liberation Organization in Washington, D.C.*

Dear Yossi,

When you wrote *Letters to my Palestinian Neighbor,* I do not think you imagined that Palestinians would read it or even respond to it. I was one of those who read it by mere coincidence and now am attempting to respond.

Aside from the fact that your book is a personal take on how you feel as a Jewish resident of Jerusalem, the fact that someone like you could see beyond the political and psychological walls is remarkable. I hear Palestinian voices saying to me, "How dare you validate this book!" But I will try to explain why I feel this way.

In the first paragraph of your first letter you write, "I call you 'neighbor' because I don't know your name or anything personal about you." I heard in those words a voice that we as Palestinians rarely hear. Your acknowledgment of Palestinians and Palestine was a big thing for me in these letters. You did not just acknowledge us, you admitted you did not know your neighbor. That affirms my belief in the power of knowing the other. This conflict will not end as long as we are prohibited from knowing the "other." This is a luxury that people caught in conflict cannot afford. They are surrounded by fear and dehumanization that paralyze them.

Your letters confirmed my feeling that religious narratives shape the Palestinian-Israeli conflict. Religion is meant to unite us; why do we, the descendants of Abraham, fight among ourselves? And for what? Is it because these religious narratives put us in two different categories, the chosen and the non-chosen? Is it because Abraham did not resolve his issues in his relationship with his sons and wives? Is it because we both think we are victims of ongoing forms of oppression? Should we rethink these narratives and try to offer the next generation of Jews and Palestinians a new narrative of shared destiny and shared values of humanity and justice?

You did your best to be honest about your fears and aspirations. I hope this will be a step forward for more difficult conversations about Palestine and Israel.

Yours,

Huda Abuarquob

*Huda Abuarquob is the regional director for the Alliance for Middle East Peace (ALLMEP)*

Dear Yossi,

We are a "Palestinian girl" from Nablus and an "Israeli boy" from Jerusalem who met in Washington, D.C., during a program at American University. We are writing to tell you about the work we've begun together.

Rawan lived half her life in NYC and the other half in what she describes as the absolute opposite of the Big Apple, a conservative Muslim village outside Nablus, in the West Bank. That is where she experienced the implications of the Israeli occupation, where IDF soldiers invaded her home and traumatized her and her younger siblings, where her mother was shot by an Israeli settler, where she first interacted with the other side holding rifles and pointing a gun at her at the Hawara checkpoint. That made her realize that peace or any other agreement can't be achieved as long as Israel continues its presence in the West Bank and its siege on Gaza.

Bar was born in the Negev Desert in Kibbutz Beit Kama, next to the Bedouin city of Rahat. Growing up, the conversation around his dinner table always revolved around peace, and he believed strongly that Israeli disengagement from Gaza and the West Bank would naturally lead to a separation. As a teenager, Bar was attacked by Palestinians who beat and robbed him. But the most important factor that made it hard for Bar to believe that the other side wanted to end the conflict was the fact that the Israeli disengagement from Gaza did not lead to peace, but rather to rockets falling around his neighborhood. From that moment on, including during his three-year army service, every interaction with Palestinians was centered around violence. Even after the army, when he was working as a tour guide in Jerusalem, he witnessed violence between both sides. During one of his tours, a Palestinian tried to stab an Israeli policeman and was shot and injured. Though most of Bar's daily encounters with Palestinians were respectful on the surface, underneath was tension and fear that violence could erupt at any moment.

We were inspired by the method you used in your book to reach out to the other side. Your dialogue modeled for us a sincere and unpretentious way of speaking. But each one of us was inspired in a different way. Through your book, Bar reaffirmed his belief that the way to create understanding of the other side is through telling his story and narrative to Palestinians and to hear their stories as well. For Rawan, this book is more complicated: Her first response was to see it as a way for the Zionist movement to justify the daily injustices Palestinians endure. But she respects your opinions and understands the importance of both sides listening to each other no matter how much we disagree. That is exactly what your book invites us to do.

As a result of your book, we decided to travel to campuses across the US and tell our very different stories alongside one another to students. This book brought us together to create a serious dialogue between Palestinians and Israelis in their twenties. We are the next generation that will be responsible for handling the consequences of the failures of the generation of Oslo, who today cannot let go of their preconceived notions of the other—especially the notion that the other is the only obstacle for moving forward. We have no other option except to create a new story.

In our program, we bring our narrative to all sides and meet with Christians, Muslims and Jews, Palestinians and Israelis. We've noticed that the audiences come with the same preconceived notions as the Oslo generation, denying either the notion of Palestinian nationality or Israel's right to exist. We stand together to talk about the issue of Palestinian refugees, to discuss freedom of movement, and to address security requirements of both peoples. Although these hard subjects are almost impossible to negotiate today, the fact that we stand on a stage together shows that change is possible. We believe that a book can inspire people to respond, but a dialogue like ours can break barriers.

Your book showed us how to develop this method of encounter. We want these encounters to spread not only between Israelis and Palestinians living in the US and other Western countries, but also to bring our approach to Israel and Palestine. We appeal to Israelis and Palestinians: If you see yourselves as responsible for helping create a new story, if you believe that the narrative of the other side doesn't undermine your narrative, then say it out loud. Join the movement.

We are working toward breaking the barriers that the conflict has created within both peoples.

Thank you, and good day.

Rawan Odeh and Bar Galin

*Rawan Odeh is managing director of New Story Leadership for the Middle East, which brings emerging leaders from Israel and Palestine to Washington, D.C., every summer. She has a BA in accounting from An-Najah National University.*

*Bar Galin is director of Israeli programming for Hillel at American University. He has a BA in history from the University of Haifa and is a licensed tour guide.*

# Acknowledgments

My deep gratitude to:

Marie Brenner, who appeared like an emissary of the angelic kingdom and made this book happen.

Sofia Groopman, my superb editor, who cares deeply about writing and writers and helped make this a much better book.

Sarah, my life partner in all ways.

Moriah, Gavriel, and Shachar, who bring me great joy and have deepened my understanding of Israel.

Terry Kassel, Paul E. Singer, Max Karpel, and Daniel Bonner of The Paul E. Singer Foundation, for their generous friendship and support. Special gratitude to Harry Z. Cohen, for his tremendous work on behalf of this book.

Lynn Schusterman and Lisa Eisen of the Charles and Lynn Schusterman Family Foundation, for their generous support and for their friendship over the years.

Larry Weissman and Sascha Alpert, my literary agents, who helped me shape this book.

Donniel Hartman, for his friendship, support, and inspiration; for his valuable editorial comments on this book; and for challenging me to aspire to my higher self.

Jonathan Kessler, who believed in this book even when I wavered and who offered me his encouragement and wisdom and friendship. If this book has a *sandak* (godfather), it's Jonathan.

Jonathan Rosen, whose indispensable feedback in this book's early stages helped me find my voice.

Haroon Moghul, for his literary and spiritual friendship.

Tal Becker, Elana Stein Hain, Donniel Hartman, Yehuda Kurtzer—my longtime colleagues and friends in the Shalom Hartman Institute's iEngage seminar, who have enriched me intellectually and spiritually and challenged me to deepen my thinking on the issues raised in this book.

Alan Abbey, Irfana Anwer, Lauren Berkun, Meirav Fishman, Maital Friedman, Dalit Horn, Marlene Houri, Hana Gilat, Rachel Jacoby Rosenfield, Yehuda Kurtzer, Kate Lee, Haroon Moghul, Gidon Mais, Shiri Merzel, Tova Perlow, Tova Serkin, Atara Solow, Sabra Waxman, Mick Weinstein—my colleagues and friends at the Shalom Hartman Institute, who have helped make MLI a success.

Yoel and Nomi Glick, for their boundless friendship and support.

Stefanie Liba Engelson-Argamon, a blessing in my life, whose devotion and spiritual friendship immeasurably enrich me.

David Suissa of the *Jewish Journal*, my partner and brother who is always there when I need him.

Gary Rosenblatt and Thea Wieseltier of the *Jewish Week*, a blessing to the Jewish people, and who are among the first people I turn to for partnership on a project.

Dan Senor, for his friendship and guidance.

Diane Troderman and Harold Grinspoon, beloved friends and supporters.

Angelica Berrie and Ruth Salzman of the Russell Berrie Foundation, and Julie Sandorf and Nessa Rapoport of the Revson Foundation, founding supporters and ongoing partners of MLI.

Jonathan Burnham, for believing in this book.

Tina Andreadis, Milan Bozic, Rachel Elinsky, Tom Hopke, Doug Jones, Muriel Jorgensen, David Koral, Leah Wasielewski—the wonderful team at Harper-Collins.

Bambi Sheleg, who left us too soon, and who first gave me the idea for this book when her groundbreaking magazine, *Eretz Aheret*, published a special issue devoted to letters written by Israelis to their Palestinian neighbors.

Moshe Halbertal, for his insights into the nature of the sacred.

Parvez Ahmed, Ali Ammoura, Mijal Bitton, Sam Freedman, Yechezkel Landau, John Moscowitz, Noam Zion—for their valuable feedback on this manuscript.

All the participants in the Muslim Leadership Initiative, who have taught me the meaning of holy courage.

Irfana Anwer, Toby Perl Freilich, Zach Gelman, David Horowitz, Debra Majeed, Leslie Meyers, Raiyan Syed, Claire Wachtel, Inas Younis—for their friendship and support.

Harry Aaronson, Leora Balinsky, Evan Charney, Rivka Cohen, Gidon Halbfinger, Sam Mellins, Yossi Quint, Daniel Schwartz, Aaron Tannenbaum—my gifted interns at the Hartman Institute who provided research assistance.

Dalia Landau, founder of Open House, an Arab Israeli–Jewish Israeli coexistence center in the town of Ramle—whose courage and open heart have challenged me to go deeper in my commitment to coexistence.

David Hartman and Menachem Froman, two beloved mentors and friends who taught me, each in his own way, how to expand the borders of Jewish being, and whose presence I sorely miss.

My editor, Gail Winston, and Emily Taylor, for their devotion in seeing the paperback edition through its changes.

My friends Marty Geller and Lauren Rutkin at the Geller Family Foundation for their generous support.

My friends at the Aviv Foundation—Chani Katzen Laufer, Steven Laufer and Adam Simon—for their generous support.

Lauren Berkun, for her wonderful work in preparing the extensive study guide on *Letters* for the Hartman Institute.

Michal Reznic, for her outreach work to our neighbors.

David Fine, for his devotion and expertise in setting up this book's website.

## About the Author

YOSSI KLEIN HALEVI is an American-born writer who has lived in Jerusalem since 1982. He is a senior fellow of the Shalom Hartman Institute in Jerusalem and the author of *At the Entrance to the Garden of Eden: A Jew's Search for God with Christians and Muslims in the Holy Land* and *Like Dreamers: The Story of the Israeli Paratroopers Who Reunited Jerusalem and Divided a Nation*. Together with Imam Abdullah Antelpi of Duke University, he codirects the Hartman Institute's Muslim Leadership Initiative. He and his wife, Sarah, have three children.

# ALSO BY **YOSSI KLEIN HALEVI**

## AT THE ENTRANCE TO THE GARDEN OF EDEN
A Jew's Search for God with Christians and Muslims in the Holy Land

*At the Entrance to the Garden of Eden* traces that remarkable spiritual journey. Halevi candidly reveals how he fought to reconcile his own fears and anger as a Jew to relate to Christians and Muslims as fellow spiritual seekers. He chronicles the difficulty of overcoming multiple obstacles—theological, political, historical, and psychological—that separate believers of the three monotheistic faiths. And he introduces a diverse range of people attempting to reconcile the dichotomous heart of this sacred place—a struggle central to Israel, but which resonates for us all.

## MEMOIRS OF A JEWISH EXTREMIST
### The Story of a Transformation

Now available in paperback for the first time, with a new introduction, the poignant and insightful memoir from Yossi Klein Halevi, the award-winning journalist and author of the acclaimed *Like Dreamers*—a coming-of-age story about a traumatic family history, radical politics, and spiritual transformation that speaks to a new generation struggling to understand what it means to be Jewish in America. As a journalist and author, Halevi has dedicated himself to fostering interfaith reconciliation. *Memoirs of a Jewish Extremist* explains how such a transformation can happen—giving hope that peaceful coexistence between faiths is possible.

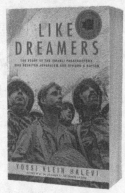

## LIKE DREAMERS
The Story of the Israeli Paratroopers Who Reunited Jerusalem and Divided a Nation

*In Like Dreamers,* acclaimed journalist Yossi Klein Halevi interweaves the stories of a group of 1967 paratroopers who reunited Jerusalem, tracing the history of Israel and the divergent ideologies shaping it from the Six-Day War to the present. Featuring eight pages of black-and-white photos and maps, *Like Dreamers* is a nuanced, in-depth look at these diverse men and the conflicting beliefs that have helped to define modern Israel and the Middle East.